MW00934217

Just Fake the Reading Log

tales from

The Self-Righteous Housewife

By

Judy Zimmerman

JUST FAKE THE READING LOG: TALES FROM THE SELF-RIGHTEOUS HOUSEWIFE. Copyright © 2012 by Judy Zimmerman. Version 2. Feel free to quote all you'd like from this just give me credit and let me know by emailing me at judy.zimmerman@comcast.net

Cover design by Rin Kurohana

Copyright ©2012 Judith Zimmerman
All rights reserved
ISBN 13: 978-1480094086
ISBN 10: 1480094080

To my three quirky, adorable, loving children:

Atticus, Grace, and Lilly.

I love you more than you can possibly know

(until you have kids of your own).

CONTENTS

Acknowledgements

I want to thank and acknowledge everyone who got me to this point: all my mom friends (the best co-workers in the world) who inspire and nurture me every day; my biggest fans, Laurent, Mom, and Coop who have always encouraged me, promoted my work, and most of all read everything I write; my brother Paul who way back in 2005 told me I should get something called “a blog”; Val Spingola who most recently told me to get my voice down in print, on paper; my sister who asks me regularly about the progress of this book; Maria Mooshil and the *Chicago Tribune* who first saw fit to print some of my early essays; Jenny Stadler who asked me for a copy of my very first essay that I read to Chapter 5; my book club which read one of my early stabs at novel-writing; my loyal readers I may or may not know personally; and most of all the main characters of this book Atticus, Grace, and Lilly, and my co-parent and soul-mate Jeff Ludwig-- I am so blessed to have you all in my life.

Part I: My Work Product

I Cyber Do

"Oh, I need to be home by six o'clock; I'm performing a marriage today," Atticus said as we drove home from the uber-nerd fest I had just taken him to at the nearby convention center. It was something about Warhammers, the contemporary version of Dungeons and Dragons. The game has changed but the nerds have not. He and his buddy had a great time watching the older kids play, laughing at the inside jokes and puns on everyone's T-shirts and generally having the kind of fun you have when you find a whole convention center full of people with your own quirky way of looking at the world.

"What did you just say?" I asked him, squinting into the low summer sun and trying not to miss my exit.

"I'm performing a marriage today," he repeated.

Now, as he is only thirteen and not an ordained clergyman, this news was intriguing, to say the least.

"Excuse me?" I said.

"In my online game, World of Warquest. I'm a priest and I said I'd marry these two people."

"Oh, I see," I said. "No, not really. I really don't see at all. What does that mean? What denomination are you? Did you choose to be a priest or is it randomly assigned? Do they know you're only thirteen?"

"You choose your characters and I picked priest. Then someone asked if any priests were available and I said I was. They know I'm thirteen. The bride's fine but the groom keeps asking me if I know what I'm doing."

"So they're not really getting married, it's just online characters getting married?"

"No," he said, growing impatient with my ignorance. "They're real people and in real life they're getting married next weekend and since they're big gamers they wanted to get married online first."

My reaction to all of this was a mixture of relief and awe: relief that he can still distinguish between real life and online life, and awe that he has the confidence to marry two people, albeit virtually.

"So do you know what you want to say? Did they give you vows?" I asked, pulling into the driveway at 5:55.

"No, I thought I'd wing it," he said breezily, getting out of the car.

"You'll be drawing on your extensive theological training?"

"Well, I've been to a few weddings."

Jeff was in the kitchen quartering limes. I informed him that his eldest would be administering online sacraments momentarily. He shrugged and reminded me that it was cocktail hour. Meanwhile, our son, the priest, sat down at the computer and calmly signed in to his fantasy world. (As we are good parents, we insist the computer remain in the kitchen to better monitor his online activity, but as he has managed to join the priesthood without our knowledge, this rule may be flawed.)

"OK," he said over his shoulder to the room at large, "should I start with 'Do you take this woman?' or say something else first?"

"Umm, err, honey, didn't you do any research for this? You know, Google 'online vows for cybergeeks' or anything like that?" Realizing that what I had mistakenly identified as admirable confidence was in reality teenage indifference and recognizing that he was now way out over his skis, I started to panic on his behalf. I began to rack my brains, trying to remember how does a wedding start? Should he ask if anyone objects (well, who wouldn't?) or was he supposed to welcome the guests (virtual and real?).

"I could run upstairs and find vows on Wikipedia," I offered, growing ever frantic as I imagined the bride waiting anxiously, her hands poised over the keyboard, her father ready to give her away with the click of a mouse. "Or I could look for our Bible and you could do a nice reading from Paul —"

Fortunately, my meddling frenzy was cut short by a little voice of reason that said, "Stop. This is not your problem. Let him take care of it." I'd like to say the little voice of reason came from inside my head but it didn't. It came from Jeff who was standing at my side. I took his advice — and the gin and tonic he had just mixed — and we left our son to perform his first wedding.

We sat on the patio and toasted the bride and groom. We talked about the virtual world we know so little about even though our children have moved there part time. And as with all big parenting epiphanies, we were forced (once again) to acknowledge that we don't really know what's going on.

As the sun turned from amber to rose, we grew quiet and our son called out through the kitchen window, "I'm pronouncing them husband and wife." I shivered as the night grew just a bit cooler and remembered a line from Kahlil Gibran's poem on children:

For their souls dwell in the house of tomorrow,
which you cannot visit, not even in your dreams.

And my son the priest said, "Amen."

The Middlest Middle Child

"Who is that girl? She has a lovely singing voice!" I whisper to my husband as we sit in the darkened auditorium watching a local theater production of *Annie* featuring kids from our church and the neighborhood.

I'm referring to the girl on stage: She's about eleven, with glasses, looks like a tiny librarian, and is holding the audience transfixed with her sweet, tremulous solo.

"That's our daughter," he whispers back.

"Are you sure? Lilly doesn't wear glasses."

"Not Lilly, the other one. I think her name is Grace," he says.

"Oh yes, Grace. I don't really know much about her."

Well, who can blame me? Grace is a middle child and as all parents (and all middle children) know too well, they can sometimes get lost in the shuffle. I'm a middle child myself, but as I came five years after my brother, I wasn't as squeezed as some middle children. But Grace, well, there's no way to put a good spin on it. She is stuck between two siblings who could suck the life out of a room let alone a quiet, introverted middle child.

The older sibling is her brother, Atticus the Wonder Boy, who is just a year ahead of her in school. He is blessed with both brains and a heart of gold. He can hold an intelligent, friendly conversation with anyone from the grocery clerk to his great-grandmother. He is the kind of kid elderly neighbors, teachers, and ministers love. When I see teachers who have had both Atticus and Grace in class, they inevitably say, "Tell Atticus I said hi," and when I add helpfully, "And Grace too?" they squint a moment, trying to figure out who I'm talking about then finally say hesitantly, "Oh yes, and Grace."

Grace's other sibling is Lilly the Hilarious Baby of the Family. She is funny. Not just kids-say-the-darndest-things funny but pitch-perfect-delivery funny. Once, when she had just turned four, I was admonishing her to be more grown-up as she was throwing a tantrum in the car on the way to Starbucks for my usual. She said, "Mom, look at me. How grown up can I be? I'm sitting in a car seat and I don't even know what a latte is."

To make things worse for Grace, Lilly is also a cancer survivor. Yes, you'd be hard-pressed to come up with a bigger attention-stealer than getting the Big C at the age of three. Poor Grace at one point during the ordeal, when Lilly was receiving yet another package of toys from well-meaning friends, blurted out, "No fair, I want to get cancer too!"

That's Grace in a nutshell: so squeezed between a math genius with the gift of gab and a stand-up comic cancer survivor that she'd risk a life-threatening disease to get a little attention. She might just be the middlest middle child of all time. It's not that Grace doesn't have many wonderful attributes too — she does — it's just that they aren't of the attention-getting variety. At the age of eleven, she can bake homemade bread from scratch, sew doll clothes without a pattern, and create art projects from nothing at a moment's notice. She is so good at taking care of her little sister that Lilly sometimes calls her "Mom" accidentally. Her talents are many but they don't often bring her the attention she'd like or the attention every child deserves — she's just too normal for that.

Which is good because the world could use a little more normal; but normal does not get you noticed. For years I've worried about this fact. I mean we, her parents and family, have always thought she's fabulous, but we're aware she was often overlooked by the outside world.

All that changed that night in the auditorium when she took the stage. I literally did not know she could sing.

Hell, she's so soft-spoken, I barely know what her speaking voice sounds like. She walked out on stage and opened her mouth to sing and I had butterflies in my stomach (as all mothers do when their children perform) and I was a little worried about how this could turn out. But out came the clear, sweet tones of a very talented little girl.

A girl with a gift! I could not have been more delighted. Grace's singing has turned out to be a true gift: unexpected, unasked for, and exactly what she needed. It has opened up doors to performing and applause. It is the perfect gift for all middle children and affords her the attention she craves and deserves. I wish I had thought to give it to her; I'm grateful someone did. Now when she takes the stage and starts to sing I am no longer surprised, but I continue to be delighted. The other two kids (what are their names?) sing too, but it isn't the same thing, those two are always on stage. The true miracle is Grace, the quiet, unassuming, middlest of all middle children, singing like a nightingale, finally in the spotlight.

Sing on sweet Gracie, sing on.

Gimme Shelter

Every six months or so for the past three years, Lilly pulls out the phone book, opens it to the Animal Shelters section of the Yellow Pages and begins her calls. "Yes, I was wondering how old do you have to be to volunteer at your shelter?" she asks politely.

In between being rejected, she will comment to Grace. "They just don't get it! They think we just want to play with the puppies like other kids!"

"Well, don't we?" asks Grace who is, frankly, not that interested in the whole endeavor.

No. That is not what Lilly wants. She wants to play with the friendless, wash the dirty, clip the long-nailed, clean the dirty cage, sweep the poop, and scrub the grungy food dishes. She has no illusions about animals. Having digested a steady diet of *Animal Planet* and caring personally for two birds, numerous fish, three guinea pigs, two rabbits, and a dog, she has a realistic, grounded expectation about what one would find at an animal shelter. In fact, although she adores all animals, she is shockingly realistic in her expectations of them: She frequently explains the dog's bad behavior by telling me, "That's just her nature." And she has no problem with any "circle of life" issues, having provided hospice and funeral services for many of them (she delivers a mean eulogy).

She would be the first to explain that shelters are not full of lovable, clean, well-behaved puppies and kitties, but rather abandoned, scruffy, poorly behaved pets of all kinds. All of this she rightfully blames on irresponsible owners. She is not bothered by the fact that the inhabitants of a shelter have issues because Lilly has a calling and it is to care for shelter animals. But no one gets that. They just think she's another kid who wants to pet a puppy. They cannot see that she has so much more to offer.

So she keeps making her calls hoping to find a shelter that has suddenly decided to drop their volunteer minimum age. She is polite, they are polite. But when she tells them she is only eleven, they nearly hang up on her. They are firm. Sixteen is the minimum age for volunteers.

That is how things went for about three years, but a short time ago all that changed when we met a very special person, Toni G., who runs a rabbit shelter in Chicago. This wonderful place rescues the homeless and unwanted bunnies of Chicago, of which there are plenty.

Turns out there are a lot of idiots who think a rabbit is a great Easter gift and then get annoyed when they realize a live animal might have a few more needs than, say, a stuffed animal. Well, when the idiots realize this, they dump the bunnies at the shelter or, worse, set them out in the backyard where they can "run free," which is code for "get eaten by a hawk or cat."

It was to this shelter that Lilly dragged me about a year ago for "rabbit spa day," a fundraising event where crazy bunny-loving people get together to have their rabbits groomed and photographed and, oh yeah, maybe take another homeless bunny home, which is how we got Suzy Q, our second rabbit. During the adoption process — surprisingly complicated for rabbits; Toni doesn't give them out to just anyone — Toni caught on pretty quickly that Lilly was not your average "can I come play with the bunnies?" kid. A friendship between Lilly and Toni quickly developed via email and they began to correspond fairly regularly, discussing bunny details that only the very dedicated bunny-lovers would be interested in or know anything about.

After a few months of this, it finally dawned on me that maybe Toni, knowing that Lilly is not just another kid who wants to pet bunnies, would make an exception and allow Lilly to be a volunteer.

So I asked her and she told me that although the age was indeed sixteen, it could be a younger person if accompanied by an adult chaperone. Now here, I should mention, that I'm not keen on spending a few hours at a rabbit shelter on a regular basis. In fact, I'm not so keen on spending more than a few minutes at a time in such a place and I had told Lilly years ago that although I would be happy to drive her to a shelter to volunteer, I would not stay with her. So my heart sank a little when she said that. But she quickly followed this up with a ridiculously generous offer — if Lilly didn't mind coming in at the times Toni would be there anyway, Toni would act as her adult chaperone!

There was much shouting and celebration when I broke this news to Lilly and within a week an appointment was made.

On that first day, all the way to the shelter Lilly was saying under her breath, "Oh yeah, Heartland Shelter, I'm too young? Oh really, too young you say!? Well aren't you sorry now. Oh Orphans of the Storm, don't you wish you could get me to volunteer now?" She was so excited she nearly binkied (that's rabbit talk for jumping with joy) out of the car as we pulled up to the shelter. I left her there in Toni's capable hands and agreed to return in four hours.

And it was there I found her four hours later, covered in rabbit fur and ecstatically happy about her new job. All the way home she told me about the rabbits she met and played with, about their often sad histories but their almost always happy endings. There was one bunny in particular she was taken with named Avery.

Avery, she explained, has been there for three years. No one wants to adopt him because he cannot be neutered. He has a heart condition and if they put him under for the surgery, he most likely would not survive. So he stays there but not many of the volunteers want to play with him because male rabbits that have not been neutered have, ahem, some hygiene issues.

"Oh Mom," she gushed. "Avery is so great! I went in his pen and he binkied, then he sprayed to mark his territory, then he pooped all over, and then he humped my leg. I just love him! He's so full of life!"

From the backseat her big brother offered this advice, "Don't go falling for every guy who humps your leg."

Lilly ignored this and began in earnest on another story about two rabbits who were saved from Kuwait. Seriously.

This volunteer date has blossomed into a regular volunteer schedule for Lilly. Toni, quickly catching on that Lilly is Internet savvy, has put her in charge of the shelter's Facebook account. So on days she isn't at the shelter, she's at home, posting photos and bios of adoptable rabbits. In addition to helping on a regular basis, Lilly has become the go-to volunteer for special events like the dog-wash fundraiser this summer and the last spa day when Lilly was a bunny-wrangler for a photographer who took shots of bunnies dressed up like vampires.

It's been months since Lilly has pulled out the dog-eared phone book and tried to find a shelter that would take her services. She's become a regular at Red Door and she's Toni's right-hand assistant. I'm not sure who is most lucky in this arrangement: Lilly, Toni, bunnies, or me.

Teenage Boys and Serial-Interest Takers

When I was pregnant with Atticus, I remember seeing babies and toddlers and thinking, "Awwww, I can't wait to have one of those!" Then one time I saw a teenage boy ambling through the mall and I thought, "Wait! Hold the phone! I *do not* want one of those!"

So I am glad to report that now that I have one of *those* in my house, it is really quite delightful.

Teenage boys are straightforward and tell you what they're thinking. They are hilariously funny and celebrate the absurd. Though they may not put a lot of thought into your birthday present, they are sweet and still wipe away tears from their little sisters' cheeks. And they can program the phone/TV/DVR or fix any technological problem you might have. As I type this my teenage boy is installing a new cooling system on the PC downstairs. Whatever that means.

My teenage boy is quirky (go figure) in addition to all those other things. He sees auras. He mentioned this quite casually once a few years back. "My music teacher has orange light around her." He is curious about everything and as an avid fan of the History channel knows something about almost everything. Lately, he's been bringing me up to speed on the whole North Korea/Kim Jong Il thing. But he's just as likely to launch into a discussion on medieval weapons (do you know the difference between a cudgel and a shillelagh?) or the likelihood that Nostradamus's predictions are accurate.

He is a Serial-Interest Taker. He has an interest, he learns all he can about it, he often saves up and buys whatever he needs for his interest, then he moves on. Accordion, ocarina, Rubik's Cube, tarot cards, film photography, and yo-yos come to mind. He dedicates hours of time on the Internet learning about these things and teaching himself how to use them with YouTube.

Unfortunately, he seldom — no wait, *never* — brings this passion, curiosity, and devotion to his schoolwork.

Which is why he was getting bad grades this spring and we were moved to ground him from his computer games and from his beloved stage crew (another of his passions; he spends hours backstage and in the light/sound booth). With all this free time on his hands, we had hoped he would apply some of it to his homework.

But alas, he has squandered his extra time on the latest of his serial interests: painting. Yes, he used his free time and hard-earned money to passionately pursue this. He saw the now-deceased Bob Ross on PBS. (In case you do not know who this is, I will explain: He is an extremely odd, charismatic guy who teaches people to paint on TV.) Bob Ross believed anyone can paint. Atticus believes that too. So while he was supposed to be spending this spring raising his math grade, he's been standing next to the computer (he downloaded the show), paintbrush in hand, following Bob's direction.

So if you have a baby boy and are not so sure about the whole teenager thing, don't worry. It will be great. He will have his own interests and passions even if he doesn't have good grades. And like all children, if you let him, he will show you a world you did not know exists.

And if you're lucky, you might get some new paintings for the living room.

Grace-ful

Yesterday I walked into the kitchen to find Grace jumping up and down and flinging popcorn out of an open bag all over the kitchen.

"What in hell are you doing?" I asked.

She stopped and giggled and came out from behind the counter. I could see then that she was hopping on one leg, trying to dislodge a piece of string stuck to her sock. She didn't realize she was doing all of this while holding an open snack bag in one hand, thus the raining popcorn.

I wish I could say I'd never seen anything so silly but this kind of thing happens to Grace all the time. When she is around, liquids spill, glass breaks, things fall over, especially her.

It is the supreme irony that we named her Grace.

Once, before I had children, I watched a family member tease a child for being clumsy. I was appalled. Of course a child will become clumsy if you tell her she is. Then I had Grace. Now I know that some people just are. They just are incredibly clumsy. If you have a family of three or more kids, ask the mom. She's got one. The spiller, the breaker, the tripper.

We once went out to dinner with friends and all their children and all of ours. As we were starting to sit down, a glass of water in front of their son (the spiller in that family) just fell over in surrender. I swear he was nowhere near it nor did he bump the table and still, incredibly and inexplicably, it tumbled over. While we all blinked in surprise his family just shook their heads and said that happens all the time with him.

This stuff happens so frequently around us too that we have coined the phrase "a Grace move." Because it is true — she really isn't clumsy; it's just that she does incredibly foolish things that test the laws of physics and gravity on a regular basis. Like trying to pour sugar from the bag into the bowl without a funnel. Or trying to pour the ketchup into the bottle six feet from the sink. You get the idea. If you study her carefully, you can see the disaster she is about to make.

This reminds me of another one of her nicknames, the Master of Disaster. Every time she opens a small container of applesauce, she manages to spill it on herself, yet not once does it occur to her to take a preemptive walk to the sink and open it there or, minimally, to open the applesauce in a direction facing away from herself.

Although, as I write this, I have to remember times when she really did not do anything that looked foolhardy yet it still resulted in a mishap. Like the time she opened a piece of candy in an elevator in our hotel in Rome and somehow it flew out of her hand, arced, and managed to fall straight down and through the crack between the door and floor leading to the elevator shaft. Really. You could never do that if you tried. If you randomly threw a piece of candy into the air in an elevator 427 times, not once would it fall into that tiny crevice. But without even trying Grace nailed it.

So if you have one of those kids, just try to relax and enjoy the eccentricity and uniqueness of your child. Really. And when she drops an entire gallon of milk on the floor of the local convenience store while you are waiting for her in the car outside, do what I did — slouch down in the seat and pretend you don't know her.

Birth Order

Due to a complete lack of planning and foresight on my part, I have two children who are just a year apart in school. Atticus started his sophomore year today while Grace started her freshman year. These two children of mine, born a mere nineteen months apart, are as different as two people can possibly be.

They say (you know, *they*) that birth order influences our personalities perhaps more than anything else and these two kids exemplify that. Given they were born so close in age to the same parents, and raised in the same house, and attend the same schools, it is incredible they can be this different, but I know from talking to other moms that this is quite the norm, not the exception.

Having two kids so different but living basically the same life can be somewhat discombobulating to me. Nowhere is this more apparent than their school experience. It's like they're going to two completely different schools in different towns or maybe different countries. But no, it's just the way they approach it that's different. Here are a few examples:

School-supply shopping: Atticus takes the crumpled list out of his pocket, scans it and says, "Let's see, I don't really need this. I can get this later. *Ha,* they never really use that. Umm, OK, I need a few spiral notebooks." We are out of Staples in ten minutes.

Grace pulls the form out of her folder marked Supply List and with the pen she has chosen for this project begins with the first item on the list. When she cannot find the exact brand and color the school suggests, she grows very agitated. It takes me some time to convince her that it will be OK and only when I promise to go to other office supply stores does she move on to the next item on her list. She chooses pocket folders and spiral notebooks with girly designs that match. They have to match. She carefully checks each item off the list. In order. We cannot leave Staples until she is done. This takes over an hour.

School clothes: Grace had the first-day-of-school outfit picked out last week and a secondary first-day-of-school outfit picked out for freshman orientation. She took photos of them and sent them to her friends so they could all vote on them. She modeled them for Lilly who pretended to care. She has been back-to-school shopping three times and still claims she needs "more tops."

Atticus has a dozen plain T-shirts (his only fashion rule is no logos, no ads), three pairs of cargo pants, and three pairs of jeans. He had them left over from last year; they still fit so he's good to go. Now, you are thinking, "Well, of course, he's a boy." But really his indifference to clothing goes beyond this normal boy thing. He really, really doesn't care. He once grabbed the jeans that I had mistakenly put on top of the pile of clothing in his room, put them on, and did not notice they were his sister's. It was not until fourth period when one of his frenemies pointed out ever so helpfully, "Dude, you're wearing girl pants" that he even realized it. He looked down, shrugged, and said, "So what." He was in the seventh grade, not exactly an age when most of us are able to shrug off wearing our sister's pants. But there you have it. He is, after all, the Buddhist among us.

Study habits: Grace comes home from school, gets herself a healthy snack, goes to the kitchen table and starts her homework. She works until it is all done. Then she does homework for stuff due later in the week. Then she studies for tests that will be given in a few weeks.

She stops for dinner. Then she studies some more. She gets all As.

Atticus comes home and gets a snack, tells me he has no homework, goes to the computer and does not get off until bedtime. He does not get all As.

I did not even know they gave out homework in middle school until Grace got there and had the exact same teachers as Atticus.

Freshman orientation: Grace goes to any and all orientations that are offered. This despite the fact that her big brother tells her that most of them are repetitious and you will get all the information you need several times over. She finds her locker and practices opening and closing it. She memorizes where it is relative to her first and last classes. She makes sure she has her schedule with her at all times. She considers writing it in Sharpie on her hand in case she loses it.

Last year Atticus skipped the first of the two orientations they offered. He was not worried. He passed on using the locker they assigned him: “It’s too far from my classes; I’ll just carry everything.” Umm, winter coat? No worries, he just won’t wear one. On the first day of his freshman year in high school, he arrived and realized he did not have his schedule. (At this point, I apologize for the nightmare you are sure to have tonight just thinking about that. I know I've had several, and so has Grace, over the past year.) Did this bother Atticus? Not so much. He just shrugged, found someone he knew was in his first period and said, "Hey what room do we meet in?" and got through the day like that.

Today those two loves of my life will come home after having both had their first day of school. Grace will tell me lots of stories about the first day, share some of the horrors like broken backpack straps and lost IDs. She will talk about the different teachers and what she had in the cafeteria. When she's done, she will make herself a fruit smoothie and start on her homework.

Atticus will come in, answer my question with a "It was great," grab a cookie, and go to the computer. Strangely, he will not have any homework.

The oldest child and the second child. They inhabit two completely different worlds. I'm always grateful to be a part of both.

Pastor Kristen and the *New York Times*

When we took a family vacation to Spain in '08, we had to fly on Friday the 13th and Lilly was convinced the plane was going to crash. Lilly is incredibly superstitious, has an overactive imagination, and is more than a little bit morbid. She went online and picked out her casket. It was a cute little thing with a teddy bear on it. She packed reluctantly, pointing out that she would never get to wear those clothes anyway.

When she gets like this no amount of logic or reason can dissuade her from her morbid thoughts. Maybe having cancer at the age of three makes you this way. Maybe she would be this way anyway. I don't really know. When she was seven, she was obsessed with "What happens when we're all dead and the world ends?" This bothered her so much I finally made her talk to our minister. I don't know what that wonderful Pastor Kristen said, but after an hour in her office, Lilly stopped worrying about the end of the world.

Until lately, because now the news and Internet are full of this "end of the world in 2012" crap that's been floating around. I tried reason, pointing out that the end of the world has been predicted many, many times and it has not happened yet. Then that damn movie came out. "Why did they make a movie about it if it isn't going to happen?" she wanted to know. I pointed out that most things in movies don't really happen like old men floating in houses held up by helium balloons going to South America. She was not reassured.

It probably does not help that sometimes, having run out of logic and reassurance, I tend to resort to sarcasm. Like last night when she brought it up again and I said, "Hey do we have an actual date on the end of the world?" Yes, Atticus informed me, it is December 21, 2012. "Awesome! I don't have to buy any Christmas presents. I could tell you I bought a pony but I won't actually have to deliver."

Lilly countered, "You don't care if the world ends in three years because you're old! But I just got here." I had to explain I was kidding because I'm not worried about it. I tried to enlist some help, turning to Atticus who, as a Serial-Interest Taker is well-versed in this kind of thing. "Tell your sister. The Mayans did not predict the future."

"Well," he said, "they did accurately predict World War II." This sent Lilly screaming from the room to say goodbye to her rabbit.

Luckily, I am very happy to report that thanks to my beloved *New York Times*, we put an end to all the nonsense this morning because today they published an essay titled “Is Doomsday Coming? Perhaps, but Not in 2012.” In it, the author assures us that according to NASA and other reliable sources, there is no evidence that the Mayan prediction will come true. I made Lilly read the whole article as she ate her eggs. She kept quoting the happy news: “Hey, NASA says so!” and “This scientist says, ‘Most of what’s claimed for 2012 relies on wishful thinking, wild pseudoscientific folly, ignorance of astronomy and a level of paranoia worthy of ‘Night of the Living Dead’.” After she tripped over the word pseudoscientific, she chuckled out loud.

She asked if she could cut out the article and take it to school. “I’m going to show it to all those crazy kids who are scared,” she said, conveniently ignoring the fact that until ten minutes ago she was one of those crazy kids.

And so I sent her off to school, relieved for the first time in months that the world will not end any time soon, and I felt good too knowing that Pastor Kristen and the *New York Times* have got my back.

The Buddhist Takes a Taxi

Last month Atticus took his journey to the Catskills to attend a Buddhist retreat. This seemed like a totally reasonable excursion last February when he first asked if he could go on a retreat in France. No, I told him, France is a nice place to go for croissants and sidewalk cafes and to get treated rudely, but it is not where you go for a Buddhist retreat. You should go to Bali or Thailand or something, but since that is a little far and a lot out of our budget you should find something in the States.

Which he did — in the Catskill Mountains a few hours outside of Manhattan. But how will you get there? I asked. "No biggie," he assured me. "I will fly into NYC and take a bus out. There's one that goes directly to the monastery; I can do this alone."

Jeff and I mulled this over and decided it was reasonable. So we said OK but when he went to sign up, he found out he had to be eighteen or older to attend. We made a few inquiries to find out if they would make an exception. He was interviewed over the phone for about a half hour by a senior monastic (who no doubt wanted to make sure this kid knew what he was getting into) and then he was declared fit to attend. So now, I thought, he's good to go.

But as the date to attend the retreat grew closer, I began to second-guess my decision to allow my fifteen-year-old to fly into LaGuardia, take a taxi to the Port Authority and find a bus into the Catskills. He's no stranger to travel, he's comfortable in major cities, but after all, he is only fifteen. So I came up with an alternate plan. Together we would fly into Albany. From there I would rent a car and drive him into the mountains and make sure I liked the looks of the place. After that I would abandon him — I mean leave him there — and he would take a bus back to the Albany airport and fly home alone when he was finished. I chose Albany because it seemed a lot more negotiable than LaGuardia and was about the same distance as NYC from the monastery.

Anyhoo, that is what we did and it all went very smoothly on the way there. Oh sure, the people at the monastery did look at me kind of funny when they asked where I would be staying during the retreat and I said Chicago. But other than that it went fine. And he stayed and had a wonderful time despite the fact that he had forgotten to pack bug spray, shampoo, and soap. After five days it was time to get himself home.

He had to catch two buses to get to the airport. I had warned him that if he missed the second bus he was kind of screwed because if he waited for the next bus he would miss his flight and I really did not have a plan B for him. I gave him a wad of cash and told him he'd just have to wing it if that happened. Of course, that is what happened.

He got on the first bus just fine but, unfortunately, it was late, which caused him to miss the second bus. So there he was in Kingston, N.Y., about an hour from the airport. Did I mention he was in the Catskills? It's a bit, umm, rustic and remote there. But, he took matters into his own capable Buddhist hands. He went out front and looked for a cab. He found one being driven by an old Indian man with a long beard and asked if he would take him to Albany airport.

"I take you anywhere you want to go," the cabbie said.

"How much?" Atticus asked. (He had $150 in cash and was praying it would be less than that.)

The cabbie sized him up and correctly guessed he was a rather desperate kid whose parents would be anxious to see him again and quickly said, "$115."

"Hold on," Atticus said and then texted me to see if that price was OK.

Though I am a big enough idiot to leave my kid in the Catskills, I am not a big enough idiot to try to negotiate by cell phone the price of a cab ride from the only cabbie in Kingston, so I texted back, "Hell yes and remember to tip him."

Atticus got in the cab, which he described as a beat up, very old Lincoln. The driver's window did not go down so the cabbie had to open the door to pay tolls. The passenger window did not go up but luckily it was a nice day.

As they pulled away from the curb, the cabbie picked up his CB and spoke to the dispatcher. "Don't bother me. I busy for the next two hours."

"Where you going? Got a hot date?" the dispatcher asked.

"Yeah, that's it."

"No, really, where are you going?"

"Albany airport.

"Sweet! How much you charging for *that*?

The cabbie did not miss a beat and replied, "You know, the usual we charge for going to Albany airport, $115."

"Oh, right," the dispatcher said, finally catching on. "The usual. Good job!"

The rest of the ride was uneventful. The cabbie was cheerful and talkative and offered to buy him lunch, which Atticus declined since he was anxious to get to the airport.

Atticus arrived in Albany safe and sound and on time. Unfortunately the plane was delayed three hours due to bad weather in Chicago, which means he could have safely caught the next bus, but of course we had no way of knowing that when it was all going down.

Besides, if he had grabbed the next bus, he would not have this memorable story, and as any good Buddhist can tell you, it isn't about getting there the most efficient way; it's all about the journey.

Put Down the Spatula

Fred Astaire was a good dancer. Michael Phelps is a good swimmer. And Grace is a good baker.

Grace likes to bake as a hobby. She likes to bake when she's stressed or when she's bored. When you are thirteen, you are almost always stressed or bored. There is not much in between. That is why nearly every day, at some point, Grace will go into the kitchen and look around, a sort of dreamy, lost expression on her face, and then she will declare, "I need to bake something." This is why you will find homemade cakes, cookies, or cupcakes in our house at all times.

Once she starts there is no stopping her. She decides to bake; she goes to the Internet and finds a recipe (with a picture, it has to have a picture); she begins to bake; and a few hours later, we will have a masterpiece. She is not intimidated by recipes that require whipped egg whites or melting chocolate. No, she welcomes the challenge of a difficult recipe. And everything she makes is from scratch because she says mixes are for wimps. Everything, including the angel food cake she made for my birthday (thirteen egg whites). She says mixes are for sissies.

She is not put off by inconvenience either. If we don't have an ingredient she needs, she gets on her bike and goes to the store and buys it. It seems she is going to the store for vanilla or sugar or eggs nearly every day.

You would think this would be a welcome blessing, all this yummy baking, but it's really not. Because when Grace cooks, she cooks like an artist — flour flies, cream spills, egg yolks splash, and chocolate drips. And don't even get me started on what the kitchen looks like during and after she uses the hand mixer. So when she is all done and holds out her gorgeous, shimmering key lime pie, the pie looks great but she and kitchen look like a sack of flour has exploded.

The other reason I am not thrilled that she likes to bake every day is that we simply cannot in good conscience or good health, consume the quantities of baked goods she makes. Did I mention she barely eats what she makes? This is a true art for her. Once she gets the recipe out of her system and has a nibble, she moves on to her next creation.

Which is why I had to do it. I had to put my foot down. Here's how that went.

Me: You have got to give up this obsession of yours!

Grace: No, please let me bake every day.

Me: *No!* You have a problem. Why don't you go do something unconstructive like normal teenagers. Go spend time with your virtual friends on Facebook. And *no* recipe swapping!

Grace: Please just one lemon meringue pie?

Me: *No!* You'll have to wait three days.

She tried. She got out her sewing machine and made some couch pillows and then a purse for herself, but when her sister refused to let her make a slipcover for the dog, she wandered back into the kitchen with that gleam in her eye. "No baking!" I reminded her as Jeff and I left to go out for dinner.

When we got home the kitchen was suspiciously clean. Usually when we come home after a night out, the counters are littered with dishes and pizza boxes. But there was nothing in sight. In fact, the kitchen was cleaner than when we had left it, which was extremely fishy. I thought I might know why so I started snooping around, opening cabinets and looking in the sink. My worst fears were confirmed when I found an overlooked egg beater in the sink. I knew then that the clean-up job had been so thorough because she was trying to hide the evidence of her crime.

I held the beater aloft. *"Who has been baking?!"* I roared.

Grace looked sheepish, "Me. Just a little."

I opened the refrigerator and there it was! It was worse than I expected. Chocolate mousse pie.

"Hey, there was no pie crust in the freezer," I said accusingly.

She had to admit extent of her crime. "Yes, I know. I made a homemade pie crust too."

After she confessed her relapse, she promised she'd try harder and she has done pretty well. She went four whole days without baking a thing, but last night, as she paced the kitchen, eyeing the pantry shelf where we keep her baking ingredients, I finally gave in.

"OK, fine. Make something for Valentine's Day, but you'd better take most of it to the neighbors."

She immediately flew into action, devising plans and going for the ingredients to make elaborate chocolate cupcakes with white creamy frosting and red sprinkles with hearts. I made her take most of them to the neighbors but there were still some left over. Which is why I just had two chocolate cupcakes for my lunch.

I know, I know, an intervention is in order here.

I'm just not sure who it would be for.

Lilly Old Lady

"You see," Lilly said, trying to explain her fascination with the candle shaped like an owl she was clutching as we stood at the endcap in Target. "It's a candle *and* it's an owl! I *have* to have this!"

Mmmm. No. I did not see. It was a crappy little tchotchke, the kind you find sitting on the back of the toilet in your Grandma's house. I said something to that effect.

"Exactly!" Lilly was thrilled I'd finally seen the intrinsic value of the object of her desire. "I *love* little old lady stuff!"

"I don't know if you should have candles in your room, honey."

She looked at me as if I were nuts. "I'm not going to *light* it! Then it would be gone! I'm just going to keep it."

Since she is only eleven, this is kind of odd. I guess there are old souls and then there is Lilly — she has an old-people-stuff soul.

I could see she really did want it, but alas, as she stood clutching the owl candle she must possess, she did not have enough money for it. I told her she could save up for it.

"But *mom*! It won't still be here when we come back! It's on sale! And look, there are only," she paused to count, "eighteen left! There's no way there will be any left when we come back!"

I assured her they would not exactly be flying off the shelf but she did not believe me. For days she alternately worked to earn money and warned me that if we didn't get back there soon those precious owl candles would be sold out.

I first became aware of this little-old-lady thing she has going when we were on a charity dog walk last summer, raising money for the bunny shelter she volunteers at. In front of us was a woman with her dog. The woman was in her late sixties, I'd guess, long silver braid down the middle of her back, gauze skirt, Birkenstock sandals. You know the look. Lilly nudged me and pointed at her. "See that! That's what I want to look like some day. *And* I'm going to have twenty cats and ten dogs."

Is it normal to aspire to be a cat lady? I thought it was something you sort of accidentally became after everyone you know dies and your rotten grandchildren stop checking in on you. I pointed out that she would probably not have a husband if she went that route. She shrugged. Whatever.

When she finally had saved enough money for the owl candle, she made me promise we would go to Target that next weekend, which we did. Much to my surprise the owl candles had been a big hit. There were only three left. "See, Mom! I *told* you these would be big sellers. You know why?"

"Yes," I recited dutifully, "because it's a candle *and* an owl."

For Christmas I found the perfect gift for her. Soap on a rope shaped like a pig. She opened it and held it aloft with delight. "Look, Grace, it's a pig *and* it's soap! We can hang this in our bathroom and *never* use it!"

I have no idea how she instinctively knew what to do with soap-on-a-rope. She's never seen it before, but somehow, like a little-old-lady savant, she knew you hang it up and never use it!

The pig will look nice in the girls' bathroom and since she'll never use it, it will last for years, which is great because some day she can hang it in her cat-lady house bathroom.

Sister Buddies

"I have a boy and a girl," my dental hygienist sighed last week, taking a break from cleaning my teeth. "I wanted another girl so my daughter could have a sister too, but it didn't happen. Everyone should have a sister."

Indeed. Everyone should have a sister and the best kind of sister is a sister buddy.

I am lucky. I have a sister and we are close but I am a little sad to say that we were not that close as children. We just couldn't have been because we are eight years apart. By the time I even have any memories of her she was leaving home for college. She has memories of me but they are more about how she helped take care of me. We weren't really sister buddies.

I know what a sister buddy looks like though because I have two who live with me. Lilly (eleven) and Grace (fourteen) have always been close. At one point they slept together so often we just pushed both beds into one bedroom, which they shared for years. This ended when Grace hit puberty (as it should) and I worried a bit that their tight friendship would come undone. Lilly, always one to notice and speak aloud what is going on, told me frequently, "Grace is no fun now that she's a teenager. She just wants to do teenage stuff and she never plays horsy anymore."

But over the past year or so they have compromised and adjusted and found a new sisterly way to be. In this way, Grace keeps one foot in childhood while Lilly dips a toe into teenhood.

For example, they have a standing Friday night nail date, in which they choose a movie on DVR — usually a Disney tweener flick (this is a compromise in itself because Grace would rather watch a chick flick and Lilly would rather watch a dog movie, so they split the difference) and spread out the forty or fifty bottles of nail polish that Grace has collected. While Grace carefully does her own fingernails, Lilly, out of solidarity, haphazardly does her own toenails. Then Grace bakes cupcakes for them both. It's an evening that has something for everyone.

Last week while Jeff and I went to the *awesome* Billy Joel and Elton John concert, the girls stayed home. "What did you girls do last night?" I asked Lilly the next morning.

"Grace put on a fashion show for me for two hours. She tried on everything in her closet."

"Really?" I know this is not Lilly's idea of fun.

"Yes. She told me if I played fashion show last night, she'd come with me to the bunny shelter tonight."

Ahhh. Another wise compromise.

Like all couples, they have their roles. Grace is the mommy: She cooks and bakes for Lilly and generally cares for her (Lilly accidentally calls her mom fairly frequently). Lilly is the entertainer: She comes up with elaborate plans and tells jokes and sings silly songs for Grace (her specialties are meowing opera songs and spot-on accents). Together they like to devise and execute elaborate home improvement plans.

Yesterday I found a list on the table with the following words: Herbal Garden, Butter Nut Wood, Lilac Rose. "Grace, what does this mean?" I asked.

"Those are the paint colors we need to paint a mural in Lilly's room. We looked them up online. But first we're going to repaint the walls."

And off they marched. Under Grace's direction, they gathered up the painting supplies and some leftover paint and turned Lilly's room from pink to blue. They assumed their roles. Grace directed the project and did most of the painting (she's no stranger to painter's tape) and Lilly entertained her while she sort of painted. At one point I walked past the room and heard Lilly doing her ghetto talk. “Yo, G! You my dawg. This room is da shizzle.”

While Jeff and Atticus and I went to stroll around the Glenview Art Fair, the girls finished up their paint job and cleaned the rollers. We found them on the couch relaxing after their hard day over an episode of *iCarly*.

Today we’ll all go to Home Depot and buy more paint so they can complete the mural Grace has designed. It will be, as Lilly explains, “a mural of a meadow so Suzy Q” —her bunny — “can feel like she’s outdoors.”

I will not be asked to help (except to buy the paint) and that is OK, because this is a sister buddies-only project.

Everyone should have a sister.

Part II: What's Going On in There?

Another Disaster Averted

Yesterday, Grace spent nine hours on a school project. Yes, nine hours trying to compile statistics on homelessness. I tried to help her, Jeff tried to help her, Atticus tried to help her, and two phone-in help-desk librarians tried to help her. But no dice. The stats she needed remained elusive.

At bedtime she was still struggling at the computer trying to find the homeless rate for Illinois. She had already found the homeless rate for the U.S. —it was 42 percent.

I said carefully, "Umm, honey, this number of 42 percent...." over her shoulder I could see Atticus trying to give me the "cut" signal. I shook him off. "Does it seem likely to you that nearly half the U.S. is homeless?" I asked gently.

She blinked behind her glasses and said, "Not really, but that's the number Atticus came up with." Oh, man, she threw him under the bus.

Anyway, as I said, it was bedtime so I began the arduous process of trying to (once again) get her to grasp the concept of cutting bait, giving up, throwing in the towel, moving on. She is like her daddy; she does not gracefully accept this part of the process.

I began by explaining to her that she had done all she could and she needed sleep more than anything right now. I assured her that even though the project was not done, her teacher would understand when she explained how long she'd worked on it. Grace was not buying it. She dug in deeper and started pounding at the keys more frantically — literally pounding the keys with her fists, her voice rising hysterically and tears coming again. This alarmed me as she had once pounded the keyboard so hard that the Escape key had flown off and we had a devil of a time putting it back on.

I tried another tack. I told her that even if she got a bad grade in this class, I would not care. This helped a little but I suspect fears of her "permanent record" were looming, so she kept Googling away.

Finally, I pulled out the ace card and offered to email her teacher and explain how much she'd worked on the project — she would still get a bad grade but her teacher would not be mean about it, I assured her. Throughout it all, Jeff bolstered my arguments by agreeing with me, and Atticus backed me up on whatever I said about the teacher (it helps immensely that he had the same class last year). Finally, our combined efforts yielded the desired result and Grace relented. She sighed and reluctantly logged off the computer and headed to bed, her feet dragging on the stairs in defeat.

As she clomped up the stairs, Atticus joined Jeff and me in the living room. He was giddy with relief that we had worked together to negotiate a peaceful end to the standoff. These scenes don't usually end so well. Usually they escalate to a fevered pitch and end when Grace turns into Carrie-at-the-prom and we all end up covered in blood (er, metaphorically speaking of course) with computer keys scattered about.

"Whew!" he said. "We avoided another disaster! I feel like it's the end of a thriller movie when they manage to change the coordinates of the bomb that was just fired at the U.S. from some eastern European country." He warmed to his analogy. "It's like we were all in that dark NASA room staring at computer screens, our ties all loosened, coffee cups everywhere and we did it. Now's the part where we all cheer and high-five and stuff, because we saved Western Civilization!" And he did a victory dance.

We laughed and then enjoyed a quiet moment of camaraderie, my husband, my son, and I, and I thought about how my coffee friend, Val, always says a little dysfunction is good for a kid because it brings the family closer, and I think she's a wise woman.

Foul-Mouth Polly Pocket

"Faye never swears, but Gary, he's got a goddamned foul mouth on him. Jesus Christ, he can hardly finish a sentence without swearing. I don't know where he gets that from," my Grandpa Kellogg used to say without a hint of irony.

I come from a long line of foul-mouthed people. I don't know when I really became aware of the foul-mouth gene I'd inherited. It may have been when I was about six-years-old during my mother's weekly ritual of unloading the groceries. We had an old Frigidaire (old even then) with a bottom-drawer freezer. Unfortunately, the freezer drawer would come off the tracks easily, rendering the whole contraption useless. My mother would have to drop the frozen foods she was lugging (a large quantity considering it was the seventies and most of what we ate was frozen) and struggle to put the heavy drawer back on its tracks. This never worked and her frustration level would escalate until finally she would get a hammer out of the kitchen drawer (kept there just for this purpose) and begin whaling on the thing, saying, "Goddamnit, goddamnit, *goddamnit!*"

That was my earliest memory of my mother swearing but certainly not my last. My mother was and is a classy lady who dresses well even when running errands. As I was growing up, she wore pearls to bathe us and gloves and hats to church. She never smoked, seldom drinks and has no tattoos that I'm aware of. But here the dissimilarities between her and a longshoreman end. If you commit an egregious act upon her house, like dripping candle wax on the shag carpet or spilling a particularly large quantity of milk on the dining room table and then wailing as you watch it slip away between the leaves, then be prepared to hear her utter a most unladylike string of curses.

Yes, I'd have to say I get the swearing mostly from my mother's side of the family. Her father, the Grandpa Kellogg mentioned above, used the word "goddamned" as conversation filler. When he spoke, nearly every noun was preceded by the word goddamned: goddamned tractor, goddamned dog, goddamned Nancy (my aunt), and most especially goddamned Anne, my grandmother and his wife of seventy years. He seldom said any of this in anger; it was very matter of fact. He'd say, "I went to get the goddamned truck fixed and goddamned Anne went with me and ran some errands while I waited." It's quite possible his wedding vows were, "I Buell, take you, goddamned Anne, to be my lawfully wedded wife, goddamnit."

Goddamnit is, not surprisingly then, the swear word (or is it a phrase?) of choice for my mother, and, I admit, in times of stress and provocation, the one you're most likely to hear from me.

My father on the other hand, seldom swears, though he too had a father who laced his conversation with profanity. I was only two when my Grandpa Zimmerman died, so I have no memory of his foul language, but my father tells a story that addresses the issue: Once, while my Grandpa was driving my father, who was about ten at the time, to the movies, Grandpa got annoyed with a slow driver in front of him who kept his blinker on but refused to turn. My grandfather pounded on the steering wheel and shouted, "Make up your mind, you asshole!" to which my father meekly said, "The Main Street Theater, Dad."

Even with all the swearing I've grown up with, there are certain words my parents and grandparents never uttered. The "see-ya-next-Tuesday" word for one and the "f" word for another. That is why these words still have the power to shock and amuse me, especially if they come from unexpected places.

Val lives down the street from me. She is the mother of three (soon to be four) children. She is a dark-haired, Italian beauty who loves her children fiercely and has no patience with parents who shirk their familial duties. Before she became a mother, she was a social worker at the high school and she has deep insights into the development of children and the importance of family, all of which she shares with me during our weekly coffee visit.

I chat with her every morning as our children wait for the bus. This morning, we got to the bus stop before she did and as we waited, I could see the front door of her house open as she shepherded her kids into their boots and coats and mittens. Her very pregnant self was silhouetted against the morning sun and she made a lovely Madonna-like figure. I smiled at the sight. Then, I heard the rumbling of the bus as it started down the street and I heard her voice rise in panic as she screamed, "Hurry, *hurry up!* The *fucking bus is coming!*" she screamed loudly enough for most of the street to hear. Nice.

Of course as parents, we of the foul mouths have to be a little careful. Some parents frown on children who swear a lot. Surprisingly, it hasn't been much of a problem around my house. Though my children hear me swear frequently and matter-of-factly every day of their lives, they are well aware they are not allowed to curse. I do have to remind them from time-to-time as I correct them. "No, you can't say 'shit,' you have to say 'shoot,'" or "'Motherfucker' isn't nice but you can say 'son-of-a-gun.'"

My use of creative and colorful words has even morphed into a game the kids ask to play called Foul-Mouth Polly Pockets. If you are not familiar with Polly, let me introduce you; she is a tiny, Barbie wannabe made out of plastic and her entire wardrobe is rubber. This is a bad combination. She is very tiny — minute even — and it's very difficult, if not impossible, to dress her. So though she is made for the "seven and under" set, there is not a single child who can actually dress her without a lot of adult help. As a parent, if you have Polly in the house, eventually you will find yourself struggling with a tiny rubber miniskirt the size of a postage stamp and tiny rubber boots no bigger than a paper clip as you dress

Polly, who like all other little girl dolls dresses like a Vegas hooker.

When this happens to me, I will invariably find myself providing an imaginary monologue from Polly that usually goes like this: "I can't wait to go out on my date tonight, as soon as I get these goddamned pants on. Now who the hell would invent rubber pants when I'm made out of plastic? The only thing worse would be if they made my ass out of Velcro and my pants out of flannel," which I say in a wee-little Polly voice. This slays my six-year-old who begs for more. I suppose there are those who wouldn't really approve of this kind of parenting. Fuck 'em.

I recently read that Harper Lee, author of *To Kill a Mockingbird*, is rather well known for her salty language. If one of the most celebrated authors of the twentieth century swears a lot, surely I can toss off a curse word now and then without it reflecting too badly on me. In fact, the next time someone tells me that "Swearing is the sign of a limited vocabulary" I'm going to point out this fact about Harper Lee. It's much better than my usual witty rejoinder of "bullshit." And if they don't like that, they can take it up with my goddamned mother.

Dog Days of Summer

Usually I reach this stage in the summer vacation near the end of August, but this year I am kind of done with them all and it's only late July. I'm at that stage when I'm wondering when school starts. As I type this, Lilly and Grace are having a raging fight over who lost the black leggings that Grace *has* to wear to camp tomorrow for their Favorite Decade Day. Christ, who invents these things? Like we don't have enough of this crap during the school year when my kids seem to constantly remember on a Sunday night that they need something for a school project the next day, like poster boards and hot glue guns and weapons-grade plutonium.

You might say my kids are kind of crowding me these days. They're in my personal space. They're all up in my grill. Last week one of them stepped on the back of my flip-flop. Again. I turned and said between clenched teeth, "Would you all *please* stop stepping on my flip-flops?" Do you know how close you have to be walking behind someone to step on their flip-flop?

I'm not the only one feeling this way. When I brought the subject up at coffee (I escaped from the buggers for a whole hour last week), Val agreed that she too was feeling a little cramped by having her four kids follow her everywhere. "One of them stepped on my flip-flop and it actually broke," she said. "And I want to know which parent started the email that's going around asking for a longer summer vacation." She was starting to rant a little. Her youngest looked up from the strawberry Play-Doh creation she was eating, amused as her mommy got hot. "I mean, who the fuck wants these little bastards around one more day than they already are!"

Exactly. Yesterday, while driving my progeny around in the shuttle bus, I mean minivan, the youngest and the oldest started bickering like my grandparents. Pushing buttons, annoying the crap out of each other, and getting louder and louder until finally I slammed the car into park and said under my breath, "Get. Out. Of. My. Car."

To their credit, they did not argue or protest. They simply got out of the car and started to walk the few blocks home, resuming their bickering and annoying each other all the way.

I wasn't always this way. I used to love summer vacation. I mean, I still love summer vacation, but I used to love nearly all of it, not just the first six weeks. But alas, the kids get older and nature takes over. It isn't right to want to spend as much time with your fourteen-year-old son as you did when he was a three-year-old. So nature turns that delightful little boy who adored you into a snarling sarcastic beast who rolls his eyes a lot. And the mommy who used to cuddle and take him on errands now kicks his sorry ass out of the minivan. Ah, the circle of life. We're right on schedule for a touching goodbye when he goes to college that should look like this:

Me: Don't let the door hit you in the ass.

Him: Up yours, old lady.

When we took a long trip to Italy a few years back, the kids got desperately homesick in the middle of it. I explained that when you travel, you will have bad days but on balance it will all be worth it. And it was. They got over their homesickness and we had a fabulous vacation. I'm hoping the same applies to summer vacation and that this too shall pass and we can enjoy the back end of our vacation as much as we enjoyed the front end.

So, here's to the dog days of summer. It's hot as hell and the cicadas are singing. My kids are arguing and I'm looking a little frantically at the calendar.

Good times.

Things That Pass for Conversation

Driving in the car on Sunday, noticing traffic due to the dedication of the new Holocaust Museum:

Grace: What are all these signs for?
Mom: This is where the Nazis are demonstrating against the Holocaust Museum.
Grace: What are they demonstrating against?
Mom: I have no idea. Sometimes they try to deny it happened. They are hateful.
Lilly: If they're Nazis, shouldn't they be proud it happened? You'd think they'd be bragging about it.
Mom: There's a special place in hell for them. (pause) Except I don't believe in hell.
Grace: (giggling) Maybe there's a really unpleasant place in heaven for them.
Mom: Yeah, with bad lighting and poor service.

Waiting in the car for Grace after her voice lesson:

Lilly: So if they didn't teach sex ed at your school, how did you learn about it?

Mom: Linda Boshoven told me walking home from Girl Scouts.
Lilly: What? She just said, “Here’s how babies are made”?
Mom: No, she told a bad joke with a naughty word that means sex, then she asked if I knew what that meant and when I said no she told me.
Lilly: What was the bad word?
Mom: You know, the F word.
Lilly: (incredulous) The F word means *sex*!
Mom: Yes, what did you think it meant?
Lilly: I didn’t think it meant anything. I just thought it was a really bad word.
(Pauses to think about it) That makes no sense at all! I mean, “sex you,” “sex off,” “what the sex” — none of that makes any sense at all.

Door opens and Grace gets in:

Lilly: Hey, Grace, did you know the *F* word means sex?
Grace: No.
Me: Well, what did you think it meant?
Grace: I didn’t think it meant anything. I thought it was just a bad word.

While eating lunch on Saturday:

Mom: I heard on the radio that those Navy Seals were such good sharpshooters that they dropped all three pirates without harming the parrots on their shoulders.
Lilly: Did they really have parrots?
Atticus: No, it's a joke.
Lilly: Oh. Ha, ha.
Mom: If I were a modern-day parrot, I would totally wear a fake pirate on my shoulder.
Atticus: I think you said that backwards.
Lilly: No, I like it the way mom said it. If I were a parrot, I would wear a fake pirate under me.
Mom: That is really hard to say: pirate parrot pirate parrot.
All three kids: Parrot pirate parrot pirate parrot pirate...

While driving everyone home from a fast-food run:

Mom: That looks like a pimp car (observing really old Cadillac in the Target parking lot with very unpimplike old man at the wheel).
Lilly: What's a pimp?

Mom: A pimp is a man who is the boss of prostitutes. Prostitutes are women who sell their bodies for money. And pimps dress a certain way, umm, like with hats and lots of jewelry...

Dad: And we know this from watching TV.

Mom: Yes, (realizing she has *no* idea what she's talking about) there's that one, in that show...

Dad: *Starsky and Hutch.*

Mom: Yeah, his name was Pookie or something like that.

Atticus: Huggy Bear (he's seen the movie version).

Dad: No, he wasn't a real pimp; he was pretending.

Mom: No, I think he was a real pimp but he was an informer.

Dad: Oh yeah, maybe. He was always talking to the one guy...

Mom: Yeah, wait, what were the names of those two lead guys in that show?

Dad: Umm, what were their names?

Atticus: That would be Starsky and Hutch.

Mom: (laughing hysterically at herself) *Oh, my God, I cannot believe I just said that!*

Atticus: (with pitch-perfect teen exasperation in his voice) Morons.

In the sunroom where all serious child/parent conferences take place. Atticus is trying to convince us he should take a summer class, which is what all the overachieving kids do around here in order to give themselves a little breathing room during the school year.

Mom: You're only young once, why do you want to spoil it with school?
Dad: Think of all that down time you're giving up.
Atticus: Please, Mom and Dad, let me take chemistry.
Jeff: Well, OK, but if you're going to take that class, we want you to apply yourself.
Atticus: Yeah, I know.
Jeff: So you should, you know, stay out of the "C-hood." And kind of shoot for at least the "B-ville." And really, we'd like you to keep it in the "A-ness." (*At which point he had to stop talking because all three kids and I were laughing so hard he couldn't continue.)*

At the breakfast table, I am wearing my Obama T-shirt as a pajama top. It has his head and shoulders and the words "Obama 2008" on it. Because it is my pajama top, I am not wear undergarments with it. Lilly comes in and gets herself a bowl of cereal in silence, then does a spot-on imitation of our president:

Lilly: Look, umm, I'm just saying, if you are going to wear that and your breasts are resting on my shoulders, umm, you should at least think about wearing a bra and bring those things up to my ears.

Sitting in the living room reading the paper on a Sunday morning:

Mom: Lilly, I hurt my back in yoga and I can't bend over to clip my nails. Would you do it for me? Now answer this very carefully as it is a test of your love for me.
Lilly: Not in a million years.
Mom: But what if everyone in the world died but you and me and my arms fell off? Then would you cut my nails?
Lilly: If all that happened, I think we'd have bigger things to worry about than your toenails.

Driving around my home state of Michigan, visiting relatives:

Mom: Did you know you're never more than six miles from a body of water in Michigan?

Lilly: Yeah, you told us that.

Mom: Oh, sorry. I guess I repeat myself sometimes. What else do I say a lot? If you tell me, I can stop saying it.

Lilly: (pauses a moment to consider) You say, "Make me a cosmo"; "Can't you get a ride?"; and "I'm going to take a nap now."

Mom: Actually, what I say is "Cosmo me." But I can't argue with the other two.

Friday Night Life

Atticus is a freshman this year and we are horrified to find ourselves reliving our high school years vicariously. Last Friday he wanted to go to the football game. He was meeting some friends there so he needed a ride. As we drove, Jeff cheerfully recalled his years of playing on the old gridiron, and I talked about being in the marching band as we shared a tiny bit of the excitement of a Friday night football game. It started raining and this was cause for alarm for Jeff. The following conversation ensued:

Dad: Hey, it's raining. Do you want to take one of my umbrellas?
Atticus: (*can't respond, he's laughing so hard*)
Mom: Good Lord! Would you have taken an umbrella to a football game?
Dad: (*catching himself*) Oh, right, no one has an umbrella. Well, do you want me to stop at Walgreens and we'll get a rain poncho?
Mom: (*laughing too hard to speak*)
Atticus: Dad! A rain poncho?

Dad: (*thinking he's used the wrong word*) Oh, you know, a slicker.

(*Atticus and I now doubled over laughing*)

Atticus: Dad, I'm pretty sure no one has worn a slicker since 1952.

Mom: You might as well offer him some galoshes or rubbers.

Dad: OK, OK.

Mom: So, you're meeting some friends in the marching band?

Atticus: Yeah. They said the band parents put up caution tape around the band so the non-bandies can't try to mingle with them.

Dad: Oh yeah, that's a real concern. People rushing the marching band.

Mom: Caution tape? Like it says "Caution, band nerds"?

Atticus: I have no idea what those crazy parents are worried about. But I'll just sit on one side of the tape and Joanne will be on the other.

Joanne?

Dad: OK, where should I drop you?

Atticus: Here's good. (*opens door as it begins to rain harder*)

We watch as he lopes off into the rainy night, coatless, outlined by the giant lights of the football field. Two girls wearing not enough clothing with their lovely lady humps hanging out walk past the car and I resist the urge to shout, "Stay away from my little boy, you whores!"

We drive off, heading to our favorite restaurant for a martini and a steak. We'll valet park and stay nice and dry while Atticus gets soaked in the stands watching a game he doesn't really care for and eating a hotdog, sitting next to Joanne with caution tape between them.

I know who's having more fun, and it's not us.

Raucous Laughter

A few summers ago we took a three-week-long family vacation to Tuscany. It was before the recession, obviously. We rented a villa smack dab in the middle of the Tuscan countryside and in those three weeks only ventured out every few days to see Pisa or Florence as I quickly learned my three progeny were much more interested in sun, pool, Italian food, and relaxing than they were in ancient Italian art and architecture.

The awesome thing about Tuscany is that everywhere you turn the scenery looks just like you hoped it would. You don't have to go to some magic hillside and crane your neck just to see a breathtaking landscape of rolling hills and olive trees and Italian villas — no, they really are everywhere for miles and miles and miles.

The kids quickly adapted to paradise (who wouldn't) and our daily excursion into the tiny village of Montaione for gelato was their favorite part. Jeff and I also adapted to the wonderful custom of an adult beverage while the kids had gelato since the local bar was also the local gelato parlor. As the proprietor would pass the last gelato to my youngest, he would then turn to me and hand me a glass of liqueur and say "*Un Limoncello por la mama*!" What a great country.

All too soon it was time for Jeff to go home to "get the money" as Lilly once said about his job. And off he returned to work leaving me to enjoy two more weeks in Italy. My friend Beth came to replace him and help me take care of the kids.

At night the sun did not go down until nearly ten and Beth and I would sit out by the pool drinking Moretti and telling the same joke, "Would you like more, Eddy?" as we handed each other a fresh beer. Afterward, we'd go up to the villa and play poker with the kids while battling the bugs that liked to fly in the screenless windows at night.

One night as we sat playing poker, tired from a long day in the sun, we heard a distant burst of loud laughter. It was kind of a quiet night for us and I have to admit we all looked up rather jealously to see who was having so much fun without us. Going out into the driveway we could see off in the distance, atop yet another gorgeous hill and just outside yet another Italian villa, a large family drinking wine and laughing. I sort of wished we could join them but said nothing.

We went back in to finish our rather listless game of poker, interrupted only by the frequent bursts of laughter. After some time it was Lilly (as it so often is), who was seven at the time, who put our thoughts into words so well by saying, "Look, they're really having more fun than us and I can't stand that. So at the count of three I want to hear some good raucous laughter. 1-2-3!" and we all burst out into loud, fake, but raucous laughter. She had timed it to come almost immediately after the last burst from atop the hill and we noticed it seemed to quiet them down for a bit. As we finished the game she called for more raucous laughter three or four more times and this was the ritual we followed for the rest of the trip.

Since that time she often calls on us for raucous laughter (or one of us will) when we're faced with this situation because if there is one thing my family hates, it's the thought that someone is having more fun than we are, or worse, that someone knows they are having more fun than we are.

So if you ever go by our house and hear a burst of raucous laughter, there's something you should know: most of the time we really are having fun, but some of the time we're just faking it.

Dating!

The waiter circles back for the third time to check on Jeff and me. We have been deep in conversation for some time so he says politely, "Do you have any questions?"

"Yes," I say looking up from Jeff, "Is our fourteen-year-old daughter too young to date?"

"Hmm, does her boyfriend drive, or do you have to drive them everywhere?"

"He's sixteen but doesn't have a license yet. We have to drive."

"Well, that's not dating, that's a playdate. Here's the wine list," he says and leaves us.

Yes, Grace, my freshman has a boyfriend--Billy, a junior--and love is in the air. This has caught us completely off guard. We know just the kind of boy Lilly, our eleven-year-old, likes (short, muscular, dark, and slightly bad-boy). Fifteen-year-old Atticus has had girlfriends and friends who are girls since sixth grade. But Grace never discusses boys--not even the movie star kind.

For some ridiculous reason, I thought because I was a late bloomer my daughter would be too. Silly me.

It's thrown the whole household off a little. Atticus mentioned that he saw Billy in school and wasn't sure how to react. "We made awkward eye contact," he said. Jeff seemed to turn into a bit of a Neanderthal dad saying, "I need to meet this boy before you go out with him!" I'm not sure what to do.

Only Lilly is sure of her supporting role. Over spring break, Grace and Billy did something every day. By Thursday they had run out of ideas.

"Mom, what should Billy and I do today?" I had no idea.

Lilly jumped in, "Well let's see, you've been to the movies, had a picnic, walked around Lake Glenview, and he helped paint your bedroom. If this were a Disney movie, today would be either wash-the-car-and-spray-each-other-with-the-hose, or have-a misunderstanding-and-get-in-a-fight-day. You could have a misunderstanding about me. Maybe Billy is threatened by our relationship."

"Thanks, but I think we'll just go to the park and he can push me on the swings," Grace replied.

When he came over one day to watch a movie in the basement, I realized just how little I understood what my role was. "Lilly, go downstairs and make sure everything's okay," I said.

She looked puzzled, "What do you mean?"

"You know, spy on them and see if they're kissing or something."

"Well, aren't they supposed to be kissing?" she said reasonably.

"Umm, well, ummm," I mumbled and again I realized I was in the weeds on this.

In the end I just went down every half hour or so (the "or so" is key--predictability renders the exercise useless) and asked if they wanted a snack or something. I figured that somewhere between leaving them alone with a bottle of wine and candles and sitting between them like a human bundling board (look it up) lies my role.

So that's what's going on around here. Grace is twitterpated, Atticus feels uncomfortable, Lilly is coaching, and Jeff and I are so clueless we're reduced to asking single waiters at Wildfire for parenting advice.

Part III: Allow Me to Translate

Playdate Speak

If a visiting child has stayed at your house through not one, but two, meal times without a phone call from home, you can pretty much assume that mom is gone for the weekend and has left dad in charge. Dads do not know some of the subtler aspects of the mom/kid/playdate world. They are all about the status quo and see no need to call the neighbor's house to ask a few subtle questions to find out if little Madison has overstayed her welcome.

They do not know that you are supposed to call and say, "Hi, how are things going over there?" And they probably don't know that even if the mom says, "Oh, fine" it doesn't matter at all. What matters is *how* she says "Oh, fine." Based on the tone of voice you are then able to determine if "Oh, fine" meant "the girls are having a blast playing quiet games together," or if it really meant "I may murder your obnoxious child if she has to stay here one more minute," or something in between. No, dads are not aware of any of this (nor for that matter are any moms who might be a little Asperger-y.)

Conversely, dads might not even notice if their son has a playdate who has far outstayed his welcome and will thus continue to feed any and all children in the home as needed without once thinking, "Why on earth doesn't the mother come get this kid?"

I know at our house, Jeff is aware that there are some unwritten playdate rules but he is also not that interested in learning them. Sort of like watching a cricket game; it appears that those playing know the rules but it doesn't much interest you. Still, he's a good sport and gives it a try when called upon.

Take the other night when I was going out for dinner with friends. As I left the house, Lilly looked at me with panic and said, "But you can't go! I need to set up a playdate!" I pointed out to her that the man sitting at the kitchen counter, her father, who runs a midsize company, was probably capable of taking care of that. He nodded affably — yep, he could do that. So I set off for dinner knowing that the issue was in competent hands.

The problem was, I forgot that this was a *first-time* playdate, which has a certain decorum attached to it because you need to assure the mother who has never met you that you are responsible and on top of things so she can leave her child at your house without worrying that said child will come to harm.

The next morning I asked how it went. According to eyewitnesses, here is how it looked:

First Lilly called her friend and invited her to play next week. Kate said yes and at this point, as is custom, handed the phone to her mom to finalize/authorize the transaction. Lilly handed the phone to Jeff who at that moment realized he did not, in fact, know how to set up a playdate. There was a protracted silence on both ends of the line and finally Jeff said, "Hello, Kate's mom?"

"Yes?"

"Um, I guess we're setting up a playdate. Bear with me, I don't usually do this."

Kate's mom laughed nervously as she realized she'd been stuck talking to the second-in-command. "Oh, that's alright," she said.

"OK, let's see — what do we need to do to make a playdate? Well, let's start with a date," Jeff said.

"Yes, the girls were talking about next Tuesday."

"OK." Now he was finding his footing, "And we need to know how they will get home. Can Kate take the bus home with Lilly?"

Now Jeff had committed a major playdate blunder — Lilly does not take the bus; she walks to school. In fact, she has walked to school for nearly a year but this tiny detail has escaped him. The blunder? By revealing his lack of knowledge in his own daughter's life, he shows the potential playdate's mother that he is not a very involved parent, thus sending up a red flag.

Lilly, who knows a social faux pas when she sees one, smacked her forehead with her palm and hissed at her father, "I don't take the bus!"

To his credit, Jeff immediately realized his gaffe and the depth of his crime, "Oh, ha, ha," he said trying to laugh it off. "My other kids take the bus, I must have gotten confused," and he resisted the temptation to show just how much he really knows about Lilly by spouting the name of her school and teacher (which is a good thing because he can do neither) and moved on to finish up the transaction by exchanging cell phone numbers and establishing a pick-up time.

All's well that ends well and the playdate went off without a hitch, but I learned a lesson. If I'm going to leave it up to Jeff, I'm going to have to give him just a little more direction on the unspoken rules of the mom world. I'm hoping that if all goes well and he pays attention, he may graduate to being able to set up a sleepover. And if he gets really good, I could test him with a more complex transaction like a first-time sleepover for tweens with a divorced parent drop-off/pick-up switcheroo.

Human Growth and Development

If it's fifth grade and springtime around here, it means it is time for the Human Growth and Development Unit in science. In case you didn't follow that, I'm talking about Sex Ed.

As a parent, I am going through this for the third time, so here is a primer for the newbies. This is how it'll go down:

The letter: You will get a letter from school warning you that the topic is about to be raised. It strongly suggests you have a talk with your child before this happens. I strongly second that. If you do not, you will have a child looking puzzled for the next few weeks as there is much talk about eggs meeting sperm and fertilization but not a whole lot of talk about how that sperm met up with the egg in the first place.

Desensitization: The teachers, wisely knowing that some words have the ability to make a fifth-grader burst out laughing, will work on some desensitization training before they get started. This is why, if you walk past Ms. P.'s room this week you will hear twenty fifth-graders shouting out "penis!" "vagina!" then laughing uproariously. If this makes you uncomfortable, I suggest you avoid fifth grade. If it makes you want to laugh and repeat the words under your breath, then come on over for happy hour on Friday because, yes, I am that immature. This explains why my fifteen-year-old son and I are equally likely to laugh out loud if, say, while playing a word game, he draws the card and reads aloud the clue that says "I am a tool." No, really, that happened over Christmas. I snorted a martini through my nose.

The presentation: At the end of the unit, the parents are invited to take their kids to see an enlightening and educational presentation put on by a local health museum. This is pretty straightforward, though again, not much is made of how part A goes into slot B — I can't use the actual words, it makes me giggle too much, which reminds me, did I ever tell you I got in trouble on my first job because I worked on Big Beaver Road and whenever I had to give the address I laughed so hard that customers would hang up on me? Anyhoo, there will be graphic questions in a co-ed setting about "nocturnal emissions" and "menstrual cramps" that would have made our parents extremely uncomfortable. This is however, much preferred to the sex-ed "filmstrip" I was shown in fifth grade, you know, the one they showed the girls while the boys saw something else. It was produced by Kotex and was so vague and unhelpful that I left being concerned that I would have to put a belted contraption on a butterfly after it emerged from a cocoon.

The talk: Whether you do it before, during, or after the Sex Ed unit, you will most likely have to have the talk. Most families agree that dad will have the talk with the boys and mom will have the talk with the girls. For most families this is just a formality because when it comes down to it, mom will end up having the talk. Here is how it often goes:

Dad takes son out for dinner/movie/snack and to have the talk. Afterward, mom checks on dad.

Mom: So, did you tell him, you know, the penis goes into the vagina?
Dad: (*Looks horrified*) No. I was supposed to say that?
Mom: Well, what did you think you were supposed to say?

Dad: I said, "You know where babies come from, right?" and he said, "Yes."
Mom: Great. Now I have to do this for the girls and the boys.

Later there will be an enormously uncomfortable moment when Mom traps her son in a room alone and says, "OK, I'm just going to say this out loud to make sure you know," and she says it. Son will look mortified and they will move on.

So, if this is your first time with a kid in Sex Ed, I wish you well. If you go over the homework carefully, you might even learn something new, like my neighbor's husband who did not realize women had three holes down there. Yes, this does raise many questions but I really can't go into it here. Hopefully when it's all said and done you will know just what to do when a butterfly comes out of its cocoon and you might be able to say penis without giggling. But probably not.

Did Ms. S. Cover That in Sex Ed?

Finally we're all done with the Sex Ed unit. Lilly just finished it up. I was pleased to see that some things have changed since Atticus took it four years ago. The biggest change is that now, they do indeed explain that part A goes into slot B. Actually, I'm not sure if this is a true change in the curriculum or an executive decision made on the part of Ms. S. (Lilly's teacher who also taught Atticus), who after years of teaching finally got tired of trying to talk about sex when half the class did not understand the basic mechanics. The confused half tended to be the boys since (as mentioned earlier) it is the dad's job to tell the boys about sex and a lot of them simply don't do it.

Bravo for Ms. S. who decided to take the bull by the horns and tell them exactly how babies are made. And kudos to her too for the creative explanation of erections (as passed on to me by Lilly). "She said it's like a long balloon that you have to blow up or it won't go in the hole." Good point. That shriveled up balloon is not going anywhere. It's a not-so-subtle point I would have forgotten to cover myself.

I realized just how comfortable the fifth-graders were getting with the whole subject when Lilly turned from the computer the other day and asked me, “Mom, is menstruation when the penis gets blown up so it can go in the vagina?”

“No,” I answered, peeling potatoes and trying to picture my grandmother answering that question a few decades ago. “Menstruation is your period. You’re thinking of an erection.”

She smacked her forehead and said, “Oh yeah! Of course,” then turned to the computer and typed furiously.

“What are you doing anyway?”

“I’m instant-messaging Alex and we’re studying for the science test together.”

In my day that kind of talk would have gotten your knuckles smacked with a ruler (not really; it was the seventies and no one was hitting anyone in the public schools, but I wanted to say that). Certainly I would have been much too mortified to say any of the words in her question in front of a boy or type them if such space-age technology existed back then. Secretly I was thrilled that my kids are so much more comfortable with the whole human body-sex thing than kids were in days of yore.

So I was feeling pretty good about the whole thing. All three kids have gone through sex ed so all three are well-versed in the topic. I've also had the "always wear a condom — every time" conversation with all three of them repeatedly. (By the way, did you know that experts say when it comes to uncomfortable subjects like sex and drugs and why all Illinois governors go to jail that you should talk about these things so frequently that kids have no memory of a single conversation? It's just something they grow up hearing about. Good to know especially for those of us who remember in excruciating detail the talk our mother gave us — or in my case, the talk my mother never gave me.)

Anyhoo, like I said, I was feeling pretty cocky and forward-thinking and progressive on the whole thing until Saturday night when the family watched a PG-13 movie, in which one of the mean high school girls says to the nice high school girl, "I've heard you've never had an orgasm." On what planet do high school girls talk this way, I wonder? So of course Lilly had to ask, "What's an orgasm?"

Uh-oh, Ms. S., didn't you cover that?

"Oh," I said breezily, "that's the part that feels good so you want to have sex. Otherwise who would do that?"

"Oooohhhhh!" Lilly said, as another piece of the mysterious puzzle fell into place. "It actually feels good?"

"Yes," Jeff offered. "It's the part that makes you want to say yippee."

Grace looked mortified and Atticus heh-heh-hed exactly like my brother Paul did at that age.

Later in the movie when said nice girl had her orgasm (thankfully off-screen), Lilly asked, "If it feels good, why does she sound like she's in pain?"

I ignored the question.

Some things a girl has to figure out on her own.

Unless Ms. S. wants to cover that for me too.

I Speak Middle School

Today I will helpfully translate the names of the classes our children in junior high are enrolled in. Let's start at the very beginning, a very good place to be:

***Middle school means junior high**:* At orientation night they will tell you that middle school is a more nurturing and transitional educational experience than junior high. Instead of moving every hour on the hour to a new class as they do in high school, the kids move from "block" to "block" every hour or hour and a half or two hours depending on the complex scheduling grid that only a Homeland Security spy or a junior high kid can even keep track of. Blah, blah blah. If it's a school full of eleven- to fourteen-year-olds with poor personal hygiene habits and an obsession with the word "popular," it's still junior high to me.

***English class is now called Language Arts**:* I have no idea when or why this changed but I strongly suspect it is due to the propensity of all vocations to invent jargon that makes their practitioners sound more knowledgeable. Because Language Arts is "arty," it places a heavy emphasis on the creative writing and not so much on the grammar and punctuation. But that switch occurred way back when I was in school, which is why people today still don't know the difference between whom and who and lay and lie (myself included). Diagramming sentences and using good grammar is so 1950s.

***The Library is now the Learning Center**:* Now this one I can embrace a little — I mean the need to rename a library. As books are replaced with computers, it does seem a little silly to keep calling it a library. You do need a place to put the *Mulan* video you are going to show in Social Studies (not kidding) and the *Biggest Loser* workout videos for gym class (also not making that up). Still, Learning Center is a little vague — isn't the whole school a learning center?

***Foreign Language is now Global Language**:* Who knows why? Maybe foreign sounded derogatory? But isn't any language that isn't your own foreign? Whose feelings were being hurt here? And global is sort of a misnomer because no language is really global and even though we like to think that English is spoken everywhere, it's really not, and no, speaking louder and louder does not work.

Art is Visual Art: So as not to be confused with the other arts such as music and dance, I suppose. But doesn't this leave out the sightless? I think it should be Visual If Able Art (which reminds me how in church they say "please stand as you are able," which is as unnecessary as the announcement I've heard in stores: "Mrs. Smith, if you are in the store, please come to customer service." Think about that; I'll wait.)

Good news: Math, Science, and Social Studies are still Math, Science, and Social Studies. For now.

And now, for my personal favorite. The other day Atticus said he'd have time to finish his homework in PCT. Please elaborate, I said. Productive Choice Time, he said, snickering. Do you mean homeroom? I asked incredulously. Yes, indeed.

Now I don't know about you, but I'd have to say that in junior high, a time during which I made more unproductive choices than any other time in my life (with the possible exception of my last term of college, but that is an entirely different story altogether), I made the most unproductive choices of all in homeroom passing notes in the form of quizzes (How bored are you? Check one), discussing who likes whom and who said what to whom, and endlessly ranking my crushes though the list was almost always topped by junior high-BMOC Marc Hooth, bad-boy Joe Doga, and boy-next-door Kenny Gratton. Sigh. Now that was productive choice time.

So, if you have kids heading into junior high, consider yourself a little more prepared now that you've read my handy guide. I suggest you not try to get any more involved with these anxiety-fraught years and just watch as your gawky preteen enters junior high and emerges a slightly less gawky high schooler. It's my belief that with high school freshmen, as with laws and sausages, it's best if you don't see how they are made.

Award Season

The month of May in Glenview and in many school districts, I suspect, means lots and lots of award ceremonies for all our brilliant and talented children. Of course, in a world where kids can't even attend a birthday party without getting a custom-made T-shirt, we would not expect them to finish up their school year without making sure each and every one of the little darlings is given an award, a plaque, a certificate, and a big round of applause just for being you!

This means that as a parent you will get a letter or a phone call from the school inviting you to attend an award ceremony because your son or daughter has received an award for some great scholastic or athletic achievement at school.

At least that's what you think the first time you get one of those letters or calls. You get the video camera fired up and see if you can talk a grandparent or spouse or a younger sibling into going with you for the big event.

Imagine your disappointment (not to mention your mother's irritation) when you get there and find out the award is for Good Effort in French, which is an award given to just about any kid who attended the class on a semiregular basis. Heh, heh, you smile apologetically at your mom for keeping her from her Pilates class as your brilliant progeny traipses across the multipurpose room along with a dozen or so other slackers while Mlle Jones hands him a "special certificate" she just printed out on her computer and says with a big smile, "Tres bien!"

I am only exaggerating a little here. To be fair, they also give out awards to children who really deserve the recognition for the nearly Herculean efforts they put into the school year and the extra-curricular activities. The problem is that when you are invited to attend an award ceremony you have no idea if your kid is going to get a real award or a bogus award. So you go, and since you've been duped before you don't make a big deal about it or even tell your spouse because you don't want him to take time off to watch your kid get an award for being above average in Social Studies. And that will be the time your kid actually wins the school award for all-around kid greatness that goes to only one kid and the newspaper will be there and they'll want a picture of your entire family and they'll wonder how such a great kid could come from such an apathetic family.

Well, that has never happened to me but it nearly happened to my friend Kelly, who, a few years back, sent her husband off to work with reassurances that their son TJ would be getting some meaningless award only to find out that he was about to set a school record for receiving the most (real) awards. Thank goodness for cell phones. We fondly remember that event as the TJ Mihelic Awards Ceremony around here.

Of course it helps if you can crack the code. Last year I was going to the meaningless award ceremony (you're only invited to this one if your kid is going to win several meaningless awards, I have at least figured that much out by now) only to see the parents of the superstars leaving the building. "Hey, where are you all going?" I asked naively. TJ's mom explained gently, "Oh, they have the school-wide awards first. They just finished up," she said, trying to hide behind her back the stash of gold medals and award statues her son had just won. She's a modest woman.

WTF? They have the real awards first then break up into classes for the meaningless awards and I didn't even know that?

All of this came back to me yesterday when I got a letter inviting me to the Science Awards Ceremony at the high school. This is the first year I have someone in high school so now I have to try to decode the ceremony system there too. I was quite suspect of the invitation. For one thing Atticus is barely carrying a B-plus in that class. Can they really award that? Maybe he found a cure for a disease or something. So I asked him about it when he got home.

"Oh, that. It's nothing. I think the teacher has to give out a certain number of awards and our class is so lame he had to choose me. I wouldn't come unless you're incredibly bored."

"So you knew you were getting it?"

"Yeah. The teacher had me address the envelope to you."

Wow. That is an honor. Here, send this letter to your mom so she'll know we're giving you this prestigious award.

So I'm proposing an award system code that is just for the parents. The invitation to the award ceremony could have a three-tier code system like our oh-so-helpful Homeland Security threat system:

***Code Blue**:* This is a perfunctory award given to your kid because he or she has not physically harmed anyone in this class and did show up, fully dressed, almost every day of the school year. Come if you can squeeze it in between the grocery trip and the bill-paying.

Code Yellow*:* This is an actual award for only the top 15 percent of the class. Nifty certificates with names printed on them will be given! You may want to attend this and even make an attempt to photograph the event on your cell phone.

Code Orange *(also known as the TJ Mihelic code):* This is a real award. Your son or daughter not only got all As, but also headed up a project to implement an easy-to-use recycling system for the cafeteria that involves the help of the special needs kids and led the basketball team to a statewide victory. Bring your family and your camera and your video camera with tripod. Dress nicely; you will probably be photographed for the paper.

Happy awards season. I hope your children get many awards, real and otherwise!

Birthday Parties

Do you remember when birthday parties were small family events with a homemade cake? And maybe every few years you might have a party for kids in your class and they would come over and you'd play Drop the Clothespin in the Milk Bottle (because all milk came in bottles then, not just the expensive organic kind) and you might play Musical Chairs, and then you'd open presents and have cake and ice cream and then your friends walked home and they wouldn't have dreamed of expecting anything more at the end of the party. Do you remember that? You do? You must be really old.

Because nowadays birthday parties are big, big, big events! First of all you must have one each and every year. No, it does not matter if you have three or six or ten kids; you must plan and execute a full-on blow-out for each and every one of your offspring from the time they turn one — perhaps the silliest birthday party of all — until the last one is out of the house, which hopefully is before the current average age of thirty because you will feel pretty silly when your kid is twenty-eight and you still have to send out dinosaur invitations.

And the party must never, never, never be held at your home — no, goodness, no. Unless you hire a clown or a magician or a pony or preferably all three.

You must also spend a lot of money on theme invitations and decorations and the required matching "goody bag." What the hell is a goody bag, you might ask? It is the bag of goodies you give each of the guests when they come to your child's party because of course it is not enough for a child to go bowling or play putt-putt with his or her friends and eat pizza and ice cream and cake. No. Who would show up for that lame-o experience if there weren't a goody bag to close the deal?

The goody bag is a bag stuffed with crap you paid too much for, such as erasers and pencils and little cheap yo-yos that last for just one yo, and plastic rings that no one would ever wear. When your children come home with the goody bag, they will paw through it for the candy, insist you keep the rest of the junk because it is "cool" and then never, ever, ever play with the toys that are in it again. If you are like most moms I know, you will keep it around and then secretly throw it away along with 90 percent of their precious art projects that the teachers send home at the end of the year bound up in a fancy portfolio that a volunteer art mom got stuck making — oops, don't tell.

So that's what birthday parties look like now. Over the years my kids have been to parties at bowling alleys, skating rinks, and pools. They have made hideous pottery items and gone on guided nature walks and gone to the movies. Now that they are older I expected this to trail off but it hasn't. At fourteen and fifteen a lot of their friends are still hosting bowling or skating parties.

I confess that to some extent I have been a part of this. We have indeed hosted parties that were held at bowling alleys and inflatable bouncy places. We have also bought goody bags and stuffed them with junk. It's not that I didn't want to stop the madness, I did. One year I tried to give them all a book instead of a goody bag but most of them looked at me and blinked like I was clinically insane. One child kept trying to hand the book back as if I'd made a mistake. The brat — there's always one at a birthday party — actually asked where his goody bag was. Another time, in a real rebellious moment, I decided there would be no goody bags but kept that decision to myself. When my family asked where the goody bags were about twenty minutes before the first guest was scheduled to arrive, they all were so mortified,

Jeff included, that we ended up running around the house, filling brown paper lunch bags with old pencils and erasers and any other trinket we could put our hands on. I'm sure the kid who got my tape measure was delighted.

We have, I'm happy to report, had better luck with my equally crazy idea to host "house parties." The girls come up with their own theme and then run with it making the invitations and the decorations by hand. Then they invent theme-related activities. That's how they ended up dressed like mice and playing Cat and Mouse and Cheese one year. It was lovely and I even heard one of the little girls say, as she was picked up by her mother, "Next year, I want a house party!"

Her mother nodded and agreed, no doubt remembering the "house parties" of her youth and wondering who the heck you hire to help stage such an unusual event.

The Mosquito: Can *You* Hear It?

Atticus stood near the computer speakers and clapped his hands over his ears. "It sounds like Pop Rocks exploding in my ears while you have a tin can over my head and are banging it with a spoon!" I strained to hear the noise he was referring to but I couldn't hear a thing. I turned the volume up causing him to flee the room and leaned in closer to the speakers. Still nothing. Lilly and Grace could both hear it, though it wasn't as noxious to them as it was to their big brother. It was a strange feeling knowing there is something my children can hear that I cannot, no matter how much I turned it up.

What I was trying to hear is the latest weapon in teen crowd control, the Mosquito, created by a British inventor. The Mosquito is a sound audible only to teens and those in their twenties. Younger children can hear it but it isn't annoying to them. For some reason though, it is a sound that drives young adults from a room. For the rest of us adults, we can't hear it at all because apparently we all suffer from hearing loss as we age — something called presbycusis — even if we didn't subject ourselves to loud rock concerts or work with jackhammers. They're using this in malls and other gathering spots to drive those durned whippersnappers out of the place. Isn't that a clever invention?

But it's not as clever as the teens this tone is targeting, because they are using the Mosquito as a ring-tone for their cell phones, which means teachers and parents cannot hear it. This is particularly handy in the classroom as teens alert each other to new text-messages without the teacher's knowledge.

At first I found this information unsettling for some reason. I mean, sure, there are all kinds of teen communication systems that I don't understand, including Facebook and texting, but in theory, I could post my profile in hopes of attracting 1,237 "friends" or I could learn to type U R my BFF with my thumbs. But this sound is different. I cannot, even in theory, use it. It is undetectable to me.

So how about that image of our kids wasting their precious class time by sending each other secret text messages that adults can't even hear? I was lamenting this new development with a friend who wisely pointed out that perhaps some of us had wasted about the same amount of time writing and passing notes that teachers, for the most part, were unable to detect. Oh yeah. That's right. In fact, in the seventh grade, my best friend, Diane

Kleckner, and I taught ourselves the alphabet in sign language just so we could pass valuable intel to each other across the room in algebra, which is why to this day I still know how to sign "Joe Doga is a fox."

Maybe the Mosquito is just proof that today's kids have had to ratchet up the stealth factor to elude ever-increasingly interfering parents. Our parents wouldn't have dreamed of intercepting, let alone reading, our notes passed in class, but my peers think nothing of spying electronically on their children's emails and text messages. Boundaries, people, boundaries!

My son mentioned that his choir teacher, who is a tender twenty-seven years old, can still hear the Mosquito but only faintly and I was reminded of the magic sleigh bell in *The Polar Express* that only children can hear. The final passage of that book reads, "At one time most of my friends could hear the bell, but as the years passed, it fell silent for all of them."

So you see, the Mosquito isn't a terrifying new weapon in the arsenal of the teen world; it's simply a real-life manifestation of *The Polar Express* sleigh bell.

Still, I don't like knowing I can no longer hear either one.

Shopping Gene

Grace is a girly girl. I am not. Me having a girly girl is a little like the ex-hippie Keatons having the neo-conservative Alex in *Family Ties*. It is a funny fit. She likes perfume and makeup and shopping and her bathroom is completely full of bottles of mysterious girl stuff. She does her nails every Friday night and has, at last count, forty-seven bottles of nail polish.

I on the other hand wash my hair with whatever brand of shampoo is on sale. I do not like perfume and only wear makeup because without it you would not know I had a mouth or eyes. I do not like chocolate or high heels and I hate the show *Sex and the City*. I am in charge of the remote. (I may be a dude.) Oh, and I really, really hate to shop for clothing.

But Grace is a real girl and she looooves to shop. For her fourteenth birthday she asked for a shopping spree. She knows I not only dislike shopping but I am incapable of shopping for more than one hour. At that point I simply stop where I am, put down anything I'm holding, and say, “I’m finished,” and leave the store.

Which is why she was going to have her shopping spree with her friend Lauren, who likes to shop. But alas, they were unable to work out the logistics and Grace was eager to get to the mall so she had to go with me. I told her we could go for as long as she wanted as long as I had frequent breaks.

Off to Woodfield Mall we went. OK, I have to say that shopping for clothing for teenage girls has changed just a bit since I used to go to Livonia Mall with Jenny Stabenau and shop at Marianne's.

First of all there are these uber-hip, trendy stores with blasting loud music that sounds like a soundtrack for a migraine. And they have sprayed nauseatingly stinky perfume around to create an atmosphere. And worst of all for an old person like me, in one of them, Hollister — a brand name some girls like to wear on their asses with their Uggs — it is *dark*! I mean dark like a bar. When we stumbled into that store, the greeter, who was dressed like a pole dancer, approached us to tell us about the specials. I asked her for a Cosmo. She pretended she didn't hear me and told us the shorts were buy one, get one free. I peered into the darkness. Where are the shorts? Grace took my hand and led me like a blind person to a shelf where the shorts were, lit by a tiny bulb like the one over your stove. I held a pair up. "Oh, look Grace, isn't this cute? They have shorts for toddlers here too!" She rolled her eyes.

After two minutes in Hollister I declared I could not take it and made her leave. We found another store called Aeropostale. That one was much better. Well-lit. Not so loud. But it was weird because there were guys everywhere. Not guys who have been dragged along to shop with their girlfriends, but guys (presumably straight) shopping for themselves! Yes, half the store was for girls and the other half for guys. And then there were guys working there! Oh, my, how the world has changed. A young man asked if we needed help finding a size. Thank God Jeff wasn't there because I know he would have insisted that the clerk hand over his man-card right then and there.

Yes things have changed since I went shopping as a teen. Of course that was so long ago we used to just go down to the general store and order us some new clothes from the Sears catalog. No, seriously, it was so long ago that girls shopped in girl stores and guys, well they didn't shop. I don't know how they got clothing at all come to think of it because I never saw them in stores.

Anyway, all in all I have to declare the shopping spree a success. Grace got a ton of clothes and I was able to be a supportive shopping buddy for over three and half hours, which is like a world record for me.

And I only needed one root beer break.

Part IV: I Have a Life of My Own You Know

The Night Before the Night Before Christmas

When you grow up as the teacher's pet who always follows the rules and have been called a goody-two-shoes on more than one occasion and you had cat-eye glasses and bangs and played clarinet, you may find that when you are older you will have the need to rebel just a little in a blatant and sad attempt to show the world that you are not that same little nerd. No. Not you. You are cool. You may find yourself rebelling in any number of tiny ways, like not returning library books on time or not tipping a surly waiter the full twenty percent or even hanging up on a telemarketer in midsentence. And maybe, just maybe, you will like the way that feels so much you will look for ways to escalate your bad-girl ways until one day you decide to do something not just a little bad but scandalous!

Email to my friend Beth who is cool and lives in the city:

Me: Just supposing a suburban housewife wanted to get a tattoo. Where would she go to do that? Options are limited in the burbs. A "friend" of mine wants to know.

Beth: Tell your "friend" she could bring her minivan down to my apartment, ditch it behind the building and I could "hook her up." By the way, what is your "friend" going to tell her children when they see their mom has a tattoo?
Me: I ... I mean, my "friend" is going to say you have to be forty-four to get a tattoo.
Beth: See you this weekend.

It was almost Christmas and I had decided I would reveal my tattoo to Jeff as a Christmas present. In recent years I had noticed that he, like most of society, had gone from being horrified by tattoos as the domain of longshoremen to recognizing that a little ink on the right body part could be alluring.

And so I went. In to the big bad city. Since I am completely incapable of subterfuge, I told Jeff I was going into the city to meet my friends and do something related to his Christmas present. I planned to spend the night so I would not have to reveal my bandages ahead of time.

It was the night before the night before Christmas. Beth gave me dinner and made me watch a *Saturday Night Live* skit on middle-aged women who want to get rid of the lower back tattoos they got in their youth. It was funny and cautionary but did not deter me. Besides, I wasn't going for a full tramp stamp. Just something small and cute. We met up with Trudy who also lives in the city and is cool and we went to a bar for a few beers to fortify me before going to get my ink. Not too many beers, they cautioned; you can't get a tattoo if you're drunk. Really? Like all those rappers who come in are stone-cold sober?

The tattoo parlor looked strangely normal: well-lit, white tile, chairs lined up like a beauty parlor. In fact it could have been a Hair Cuttery if it wasn't for the receptionist who was covered in tattoos and had every piercing known to me and some not known to me. I wonder how she goes through airport security. She was very polite, like she was used to middle-aged housewives wandering in on a frigid nearly Christmas Eve to get a tattoo. A beat cop came in and at first I thought it was some kind of raid. Then I realized he had just come in to get warm and chat up the receptionist. Man, tattoo parlors have sure gone mainstream when cops stop by like they're hitting a doughnut shop. It almost took the bad-girl-ness right out of the moment.

I had decided I wanted a small heart on my right hip. I picked out a picture the size I wanted and was shown to a chair. My ink-man, Roger, explained he would first do it in marker and if I liked it, he would go ahead and tattoo me. It looked good and I draped myself over the chair (like a massage chair) and pulled my jeans down discreetly.

Just then the receptionist's phone rang. She called out in our direction, "It's for you! It's your mom!"

"Jesus, how did she find me?" I said with a start. The girl frowned at me.

"Not you, him," she said pointing to Roger. Oh right, heh heh.

Wait a minute, the tattoo artist gets calls at work from his mom? Does she know what he does for a living? Of course she does, she just called the Windy City Tattoo Parlor.

"I love you too," he said as he finished up and turned back to the ass at hand.

"OK, ready? It will sting a little."

"Puhleaze," I say. "I've had three kids — oo, oo, ow, ow, *ow!*"

Well, that was unexpected. I don't know why. The way you make a tattoo is to puncture tiny holes in the skin repeatedly then fill the holes with ink. Of course I should have known it hurt but I was completely surprised by how much. How do people do those big tattoos? How about those ankle tattoos? I started to breathe using my Lamaze technique. Finally I squeaked out, “Are you almost done?”

Roger stopped and said, “Yes, I have the outline of the heart.” Beth and Trudy were laughing at me. I asked them how long I’d been under the needle. “Like ninety seconds,” Beth said.

“Should I fill it in now?” Roger asked, perhaps sensing I didn’t have the fortitude to go on.

“Umm, you know I think the outline is fine,” I said, just wanting to get away from the crazy man with the needle now.

He was dubious. “It doesn’t show that much. Maybe I could do another outline around it in black.”

Perfect. I could save a little face that way. “Sure, go ahead.”

Roger finished up and put a very sanitary looking piece of gauze on my wound. He explained how to take care of it and sent me on my way. Trudy and Beth took me to the bar for a celebratory beer. Despite my urging, they indicated they would not be joining me anytime soon in my new bad-girl ways.

On Christmas Eve, while the rest of the world went to Midnight Mass, I gave Jeff his new present. He was as shocked and surprised as I had hoped.

And best of all, it's official now: This goody-two-shoes is b-b-b-bad to the bone.

Let's Tidy Up Down There

A while back I was sitting around a hotel pool in Scottsdale drinking Heinekens with my sister-in-law, Lisa, from L.A. This is one of my favorite things in the world to do and at the end of the day I had a "gossip burn" on half my face from turning my head toward her for so long.

Anyway, she was busy telling me all about a wild Hollywood party that she and her husband (my brother) had attended the week before.

"Paul was taking pictures and when we got them developed he had one of this girl who was twirling on the dance floor and her skirt was completely up."

"You mean you could see her underwear?" I exclaimed. Those things never happen at parties I go to. Hollywood is so exciting.

"No, I mean she wasn't wearing underwear," Lisa said.

"Wow, that must have been embarrassing."

"And," Lisa said, leaning in for dramatic effect, "she was completely shaved."

"Well, of course she was shaved, she was wearing a skirt," I say. I may be provincial but even I know you have to shave your legs when you go to a party.

"No, she was shaved ... down there," Lisa said, pointing at her nether regions. She loves to shock me. It worked.

"What!" I mean I have heard of those Brazilian bikini waxes that remove pretty much all the hair and I know those sluts in *Sex and the City* do that and Victoria Secret models would have to for practical reasons, but real people? No, no way.

"I tried it," Lisa said, gulping her beer and waiting to see my reaction.

"You mean you waxed?" I squeaked in horror remembering the one time in high school I had tried to wax myself and when I realized I had to pull my hair out, I abandoned the project midway leaving me to pick wax out of my pants for weeks.

"No, that hurts too much, I just shaved."

"Well, don't you have to cut it with scissors or something first?"

Here my brother chimed in. "She started with the weed whacker, moved on to the lawn mower, then scissors, then finished up with a razor."

Well. I couldn't wait to get home and share this revelation with my coffee girls. They are ten years younger than me and know all about the latest trends but I was sure they'd be surprised to learn that those crazy people in L.A. were waxing their hootchies! I couldn't wait to shock them.

"Oh, lots of people do that," Steph said after I shared the story.

"People you know?" I said.

"Oh yeah. Most people. I do before I give birth," Val, who was pregnant with baby four, said. "I like to tidy up for the doctor as a sort of courtesy."

Uh-oh. Someone owes her gynie a fruit basket.

"You mean they wax it *all* off?"

"No, they usually leave the 'landing strip,'" Steph said.

I mulled this all over for some time. I finally decided I wanted to give it a try. I thought it would make a good anniversary gift for Jeff. We were going to be celebrating our twenty-first and I really didn't know what to get him anyway.

Waxing was out of the question as it involved too much pain. So, on the morning of our anniversary I went into the shower armed with a pair of scissors and a new razor. After twenty minutes I still could not see skin. I kept at it. Some time later, mission accomplished.

I revealed my gift to Jeff later that night. In the interest of protecting a tiny bit of our privacy, I won't say much more than that, but he did like it. And he did comment that it looked very friendly and not angry anymore.

I decided to keep my new look. It turns out that much like other personal grooming issues, once the initial work is done there isn't a whole lot to do to maintain it. In short, I would recommend this. It's free, it's easy, and it's legal. So fire up the weed-whacker ladies, this trend isn't just for L.A. anymore.

Mommy's Cocktail Hour

"Mommy, you need to sign this sheet on our 'Drug and Alcohol' unit," Grace says, shoving a piece of paper in front of me and nearly knocking my martini over. "Hey, hey, watch my cocktail there!" I say. Grace giggles and I'm grateful she isn't one of those kids who protests if you have a drink now and then.

It's common knowledge around the 'hood that once they hit the "Drug and Alcohol" unit in fourth-grade science you may have to go underground with your cocktail. I have one friend who started hiding her vodka tonic in a coffee mug. Can you believe she does that? It's barbaric; the only thing one should drink from a coffee mug is coffee. A good cocktail deserves the proper glass. Are they teaching that in the drug and alcohol unit?

I look at the worksheet Grace has dutifully filled out for today's assignment. It covers the dangers of using someone else's prescription drugs. Well, I'll drink to that. I peer at the paper, looking confused. "I don't get it, Grace. This isn't teaching you a thing about drugs and alcohol. Like how much vermouth is in a dry martini? Where to go to score some smack? Now how are you supposed to learn that stuff?" I ask her.

"Mommy," she sighs then peers over her cat-eye glasses at me and shakes her head in exasperation. She's an old soul and deserves a better mother than the one she got. I sigh too. I long for the days before someone told us to just say no. I prefer to just say, "Sure, why not," and "You can just freshen this up." The sad truth is that I was born several decades too late. I want to go back to the days when mommies were encouraged to have cocktails while playing bridge and daddies had three-martini lunches. When doctors handed out Valium like mints to harried housewives. Nowadays you have to see a specialist just to get Prozac. Hell, my doctor wouldn't give me antibiotics without a full physical.

Instead of all that, I'm left with a paltry five o'clock cocktail. It does the trick, I suppose, but even that some people frown upon. They should know I didn't always have a cocktail at five o'clock; but then again I didn't always have kids.

As any mom knows the five o'clock hour is known as "the witching hour." Like the perfect storm, there are many forces at work that converge at once to form the witching hour. They are as follows:

Playdates end: Formal or informal playdates end as most mommies start to gather their brood for the evening.

Meltdowns begin: Regardless of age, from infancy to teenhood, this is the time of day the child realizes he has not had enough of something. Not enough sleep, food, social interaction, time to get homework done … whatever; he hasn't had enough and it's time the universe paid for this injustice. He decides to take his frustrations out on the universe by, depending on the age of the child, wailing inconsolably, whining until his mother's ears bleed, or sulking conspicuously, which isn't noisy but does have the effect of sucking out all positive life force in the room.

Market forces come into play: The value of the TV sharply declines as PBS Kids winds down causing the value of the Wii to incline sharply. The result is that all the children in the household will begin to fight over the Wii.

Mommy realizes she has no idea what's for dinner: This is because after months or years of trying to feed her children properly she has lost a wee bit of her enthusiasm for this task. In fact, despite the fact that she is resourceful enough to come up with a Halloween costume that doubles as a winter snowsuit, she can no longer think of a single meal that simultaneously meets her criteria and the children's criteria for a proper dinner. Her criteria are that the foods must be healthy, contain no refined sugar or flour, no trans-fatty acids, be pesticide-free, and ideally be served with three vegetables. The kids' criteria are simpler: no vegetables and all food must be white. Now if you draw a Venn diagram of these two subsets, you will see there is no overlap whatsoever. Oh, and I forgot, it should be something her husband likes to eat too, on the off chance that he gets home in time for dinner. Which leads me nicely into the next item.

Daddy calls to say he'll be late: By late he means later than his usual seven o'clock. He means well after the wild and chaotic time of day that the family euphemistically calls "bedtime." He also does not mean he will be toiling at his desk through dinner, snacking on a banana and a glass of skim milk. He means he is headed somewhere for cocktails, adult conversation, and a meal prepared, served, and cleared away by someone else. This makes the mommy a bit resentful.

These five things almost always happen at just around five o'clock. Together the fine balance of order that has been established since the children returned from school collapses like the house of cards it always was. Children begin screaming, mommies begin slamming cupboards and pots and pans, pets howl, and potted plants wither as an evil wind blows through the household. It was at just such a moment as this on a Tuesday in February (is there anything drearier than February?) that I had an epiphany. I was dumping the Kraft Macaroni & Cheese into the pot (the creamy kind not that powdery stuff; what kind of mom do you think I am?) when I thought to myself, "If only it were Friday, I'd have a beer." Then I thought, "Wait a minute! I'm not pregnant. I'm not nursing. I'm over twenty-one. I could have a beer on a *Tuesday*!" and I popped open a Sam Adams and began a new tradition.

Now when the witching hour starts winding up, I simply walk over to the fridge and say hello to my good friend Sam. He takes the edge off. I'm able to concentrate on whipping up a healthy meal (like *homemade* macaroni and cheese) and calmly and quietly referee the melee around me.

I have shared this revelation with many friends. Most are already aware of the medicinal effects of the nightly cocktail. Some are a little concerned that it is a slippery slope that could lead to substance abuse. It is my job to reassure them that there is nothing wrong with a single cocktail. Look at the French! They have wine with lunch and dinner and have you ever seen a more relaxed country? They can't even muster the energy necessary to fight back when invaded, that's how relaxed they are. I've become sort of the Dalai Lama of the drinking mom set. They come to me with their concerns.

Isn't it wrong to drink alone? Hey, you're not alone; your kids are home, remember they're the ones who drove you to this to begin with.

But I look so forward to having my cocktail, isn't that wrong? You look forward to a cup of coffee and a good dump too; does that mean you need to cut them out of your life? Christ, we live in a puritanical world when you go hunting for reasons to give up the things you love.

Besides, after having given up booze for the last decade when you were trying to get pregnant, you were pregnant, and then you were nursing, you've got some catching up to do. Remember that wedding you went to with your office mates when you were eight months pregnant and the only sober one (besides the flower girl) at the wedding was you? Didn't you have to watch as your friends, co-workers, and husband did the conga line through the kitchen, leaving you to waddle to the bathroom, sober as a judge. What you've seen sober no one should have seen. You've earned that drink.

My husband has no problem with this habit of mine. In fact, he encourages it. On the nights when he does come home early enough, he and I have a cocktail together in the living room, threatening the children with the following: "You may not disturb us unless there is blood, vomit, or broken bones involved," which is exactly what we tell them when we take our Saturday afternoon "naps" too.

Even with this threat, our youngest has managed to inveigle her way into our ritual. She found my collection of tiny martini glasses; the ones I stuffed in my purse after I sampled a half-dozen Apple-tinis that those cute little girls from Absolut were serving at a fundraiser. She likes to fill them with apple juice and join us in the living room. She never interrupts us so we let her stay.

Recently, we had friends over for drinks and Lilly went and fetched her mock-tini and sat down. Our friends, parents of a newborn, looked at her slightly amused and partly horrified.

"What is that?" asked the mother.

"It's from her Barbie Cocktail collection," I said smoothly. They didn't know if they should laugh or call DCFS.

Lilly, who is in first grade, raised her mock-tini in salute.

"Cheers, Mama," she said. I raised my glass in return.

"Cheers, indeed."

Moms in Pajamas

On Wednesday I drove Grace to school because the bus never showed up after a night of snow. As I came back down our street I saw Val out shoveling her driveway. I stopped the van and rolled the window down.

"Can you believe the wife?" I said, referring to the drama that has been unfolding all week about our incredibly inept/corrupt governor, Rod Blagojevich.

"I haven't heard the details about her, what?"

"I skimmed the complaint. I'll forward it to you. They have her on tape yelling over her husband's shoulder at some Trib person 'You tell that fucker he can forget his deal on the fucking Cubs if he won't fire that editorial staff!'"

"Holy shit, I knew she was a bitch," Val said as she leaned on the handle of her shovel.

"Yeah, but really, who does that? Who stands over their husband's shoulder while he's on a business call telling him what to say?"

We both shook our heads, trying to imagine the scenario. It was really one of the most shocking revelations in a shocking week of revelations. We talked a few minutes more about the scandal, the possibility that

Rahm Emmanuel dropped the dime and the prospect of hearing him on a tape cursing like Ari from *Entourage,* the character based on his real-life brother, and then I drove on.

As I pulled into the driveway it occurred to me that the entire conversation had taken place while we were both in our pajamas. Both of us had been wearing winter coats and boots over our pajamas, bed-head hair, and not a stitch of makeup — by the way, that expression makes no sense; makeup does not come in stitches.

This is not that shocking for me. I can often be found in my pajamas until ten or so (I am right now, actually; polar bear flannel, thank you for asking) and even on my wedding day I don't think I wore anything more than mascara. But for Val, well, she was a model in her youth. I'm sure there was a time in her life she wouldn't have been caught dead outside unshowered and in her pajamas.

I thought about this the next day when I drove Lilly to school for band and I saw a mom in the pajamas/boots winter ensemble as she helped her special needs child on to the bus and I realized, consciously for the first time, that I *love* seeing my peers like this.

To be sure, I usually see them fully dressed, coiffed, and made up, and many of them could audition for a part in *Desperate Housewives,* but I like them best this way — when they've just rolled out of bed. They look more vulnerable, more approachable, more human, and much younger. Like a sleeping child, an ungroomed mom is the sweetest mom of all.

This made me feel better about the time I went out to get the paper wearing the shorts of one summer pajama set and the top to another, my sad, post-breastfeeding boobs hanging low in their natural braless state only to look up after scooping up the paper to see my children's principal as he jogged by our house. I played it cool. "Good morning, Mark," I said. "Good morning, Judy," he said as he continued on. He never spoke of it. What happens in the driveway stays in the driveway.

So here's to all my mom friends today. If I see you in the 'hood with your hair rumpled and your snowflake patterned jammies peeking out from under your coat as you run kids to school or fetch the paper, rest assured you've never been more beautiful to me.

Part V: Room for Improvement

Not a Soccer Mom

A while back I was at a social event for Jeff's business and I found myself seated next to a high-powered executive. After she realized I was the spouse, not the employee, she politely turned the conversation to children. She started talking about her daughter who ice skates.

She was very proud of her daughter — said she could be the next Oksana Baiul, which is great because the world needs more anorexic girls whose self-worth depend on their ability to do a triple lutz, but I digress.

"She gets up five days a week at 5 a.m. to practice and never complains," the lady exec said over crab cakes.

"Slacker. What does she do the other two days?" I might be a little bitter.

"Excuse me?" she said.

"I just said, the only thing that would get any of my kids out of bed at 5 a.m. would be Krispy Kremes on the front lawn and a fire in the hallway."

"Oh, heh, heh," she laughed weakly not sure if she should be amused or give condolences.

It's true, I will never be the mother of an athletically gifted child. I've seen it coming for some time but I had to face it as an immutable fact last fall when Lilly, who was five at the time, came home from the last game of her last (and only) soccer season. "I. Am. Never. Doing. That. Again!" she said as she pulled off the oversized knee socks and tugged at her shinguards in frustration. She flung her jersey across the kitchen. With this gesture of finality, any hope I may have secretly nursed of having a superstar was dashed along with the jersey.

All three of my kids have tried soccer and all three have chosen not to go past the kindergarten, daisy-picking stage. "Tried soccer," by which I mean they all begged to sign up for, then whined, complained, and whimpered through a pathetic, torturous-for-all season of chasing a black-and-white ball around a field, killing time waiting for a snack. Not one of them actually touched the ball with his or her foot unless you count the time Atticus fell over the ball. All three have ended their seasons declaring they will never play the game again and all three have concluded that soccer involves "too much running."

We have also had similar experiences with T-ball (too boring), flag football (too rough), floor hockey (too late in the day), ice hockey (too much equipment), and karate (just too darn hard). I don't know where my kids get this bad attitude about sports. Their father was a star athlete in his day, playing baseball and football through high school.

Oh, that leaves only one other gene donor to blame this on. Well, the truth is, I'm not exactly a big jock myself. The only C I got in high school was in PE, and when my friends played softball in college, my job was to bring the Diet Coke. I did join an intramural basketball team in college, lured by the promise of beer at the end of each practice, but I had to quit because it conflicted with *Hill Street Blues*. It was before VCRs, so you can see I really had no option.

Now I'm not complaining (wait, yes I am) because I'm pretty happy with the fact that my kids go to school, go to church, and each do a little something on the side. But it doesn't do much for the bragging rights. I mean no one sits next to someone at a dinner party and says, "My eight-year-old attends Brownie meetings fairly regularly." Or, "My ten-year-old son is interested in musical theater," or "My youngest likes to play horsey for hours on end." No, this is not going to cut it in my circle where some people cannot even fathom the idea of a non-sport-playing offspring and conversations center around tales of athletic prowess and the travails of being on a traveling team.

We just don't travail, I mean, travel to play sports. We only travel on vacation.

When I told one mom that my middle child doesn't play any sports, she looked at me in honest confusion and said, "But what does she *do*?"

"Umm. You know, she plays. Like kids," I said. "But she plays really good and I never have to remind her about it."

"But with whom? Aren't all the other kids in sports?" she asked.

Well, no, not really. A few of the kids in the world still hang around the house after school, but their moms don't want to admit it. We live in secret shame. We don't even have a demographic handle.

So if I'm not a soccer mom, what am I? I have the minivan, I have the kids, but I don't have a title.

Which is why I was so thrilled when recently all three of my kids tried out for and got a part in a community theater production of *Annie*. They walk down to the end of the block where they rehearse at our church. In this role, I do *not* have to sit in a cold wet field and watch them. In fact, I'm not really encouraged to watch rehearsals. All I have to do is go to the final play and sit in a heated room, on a chair, in the dark, and watch kids sing and dance, which is of much more interest to me than watching kids play a sport while sitting outside on a lawn chair (if I remember to bring it) in the (all too often) wet and cold.

I guess that makes me a Thespian Mom. I don't think they'll be making any bumper stickers for it but it's not a bad thing to be and at least I have something to brag about.

I can't wait until I sit next to the skating phenom's mom again at a dinner party. I'm going to brag about how my daughter practices hours at a time dressed as Sandy the dog and never complains.

Finally, my kids are giving me the conversational currency I need and isn't that the reason we had them in the first place?

It Snows in the Midwest — Every Year

This morning I ran out to Target in the middle of a blizzard to buy some boots. I woke up to six inches of snow — the first snowfall of the year — and panicked when I realized that (1) the kids have a snow day and (2) they have no boots. None.

Now this statement raises so many questions from you that I will answer them one by one.

How can you not have boots in December? Do you live in Arizona?

Umm, err, no. I live in the Chicago area and I have lived in the Midwest my entire life.

Why didn't you just cram your kids' feet into last year's too-tight-boots until the blizzard ended?

Well, yes, this would be the customary thing to do, but I foolishly threw last year's boots out at the end of the season, including my own, in a cleaning frenzy.

Did you just say you threw away boots?

Yes, sorry, I usually observe the strict mom code of passing the boots on to the neighbors' children, but this batch was particularly ratty and I didn't have the heart to saddle anyone with them.

Why didn't you wait until the blizzard stopped before going to the store?

That's easy: guilt. I felt guilty knowing that the kids would wake up and see the first snowfall and not be able to go outside right away. Also, I've made this mistake before and I know that by midday, you will not be able to buy, beg, borrow, or steal a pair of boots on the entire North Shore.

So there you have it. That's why I was at the door of Target at 8 a.m. — the first and only customer since no one else was stupid enough to go out in a blizzard. The manager chuckled and said, "You win the most dedicated customer award." At least I think he said dedicated. Maybe he said "demented." I felt a response was needed,

"Boots," I said by way of explanation. "Not one of us has a pair of boots!"

I considered telling him we'd just been transferred here from Africa because only a foreigner or an idiot can be found wearing tennis shoes in December in Chicago. But I resisted.

He was polite enough not to ask any of the previous questions and instead just said, “They’re over there,” pointing toward the shoes (as if I needed directions; I could draw a map of my Target if I had to).

I bought the boots, and the half-dozen other things I always manage to “need” when I go to Target, and checked out. I was still literally the only customer in the store.

I had to ditch the cart at the entrance because the snow was too deep to push through. It took some time to schlep all the bags to the car and when I tried to pull out I immediately got stuck in a snow drift. After about twenty minutes of digging with the handle of a scraper and rocking the car back and forth I was good to go. At one point I thought I was stuck for good, like the four laughing young Mexican men in the beat-up, old car (the only other car in the parking lot — they were coming off the night shift). I was mortified to be stuck in the snow and refused to ask them for help. They had an excuse for getting stuck — they did not grow up driving in this stuff. I had to admire their good cheer though, coming off a night shift at Target only to find your car stuck in a blizzard and just laughing and laughing about it. (What is it about young Mexican men that they always seem to be having so much fun? Hasn't anyone pointed out that you're supposed to be wealthy to be so happy? Have they learned nothing from our culture?) But I said to myself, "I am from the Midwest, I am from the Midwest," until I willed my car out of that drift.

When I was driving home I asked myself, "Why am I, once again, running around town looking for boots on the first day of snow? What is it about me that I cannot think about boots until I am actually standing in snow?"

It's just that even though I *know* we will need boots by December, I cannot *feel* we need them. Especially when we've been enjoying a freakish warm spell of sixty-degree weather for a week in November. It's hard for me to buy boots when I don't really believe it could ever snow again.

I have to admit to myself that I've exhibited similar behavior in other instances. Meals for example. I find it nearly impossible to think about a meal until I'm very hungry. This is problematic as I am the one in charge of making meals for a family of five. For years my husband thought this was a passive-aggressive act on my part. He's so wrong. I engage in plenty of passive-aggressive acts, but failing to feed my family in a timely manner is not one of them. It's really more of a lazy-and-in-denial kind of act.

This went on for years — my family wanting to eat, me not feeding them — until finally I managed to overcome this deficiency. By sheer force of will, I made myself think about food even when I was not hungry. Now I think about dinner right after breakfast. Sometimes I even take something out to thaw or I put something in the crock-pot or I make reservations. But make no mistake, me thinking ahead about dinner is like Donald Trump acting modestly; we can both do it but it doesn't come naturally.

I thought of all this as I battled the blizzard on my way home from Target. When I got home I realized I had left my new, favorite, leopard-print gloves on a shelf in the boot department; the boots I had bought myself had a broken zipper; and the kids for whom I'd suffered so much were already out in the snow wearing old shoes with plastic bags over them, happily building a snowman.

Next year I'm going to make sure this doesn't happen again. I'm saying it here first: This is the last time I wait until the first snowfall to buy boots! I'll overcome this boot-planning weakness just like I overcame my meal-planning deficiency, by sheer force of will. I'm going to order boots online early in the season. I’m going to order those damn boots even if it’s a seventy-degree day in October.

But it won't feel right.

Just Fake the Reading Log

So there's this new movie. It's called *Race to Nowhere*, and it's about how some of us have been pressuring our children to be high achievers at school and participate in multiple activities—and that maybe this seems like a good idea, but it has gotten out of control, and our kids are buckling under the pressure and falling apart.

The movie is causing quite a stir among those who have been uncomfortable with this all along (me), and those who want to keep pushing the kids to further greatness (Tiger-Mom).

The movie has become a rallying cry, a call for a little civil disobedience.

Yeah, baby, civil disobedience! I'm a fan. Sometimes I purposely keep a DVD past the due date, and just say the heck with late fees (I may never see the end of *The Kids Are Alright* if I turn it in on time). And more than once I have even gone through the red light at the high school parking lot on Lake Avenue at midnight when there was no traffic and I have practiced saying, "Yes, officer, I know I did that. It was a conscious act of civil disobedience because that stoplight is too damned long, and besides, it is just a sign of oppression from *the man*."

But much braver than those trivial acts, I have allowed my kids—nay encouraged my kids—to make up stuff for their reading logs! It's true. I'm that bad.

That's right; I *never* made my kids fill out the reading log truthfully. (In case you are not familiar with the reading log, it is required kindergartners through eighth-graders in our district read *x* number of pages each month and log it. Then parents have to sign the log.) My kids would take those cursed things at the end of the month, look around their rooms and write down a few titles of the several books they would have been reading anyway and make up stats about pages read. Then I would sign it.

The reason I do this is *not* because I am opposed to reading. Quite the contrary. I do it because I think it is ridiculous to require kids to document something they should just be doing anyway like eating, breathing, and reading.

And I am thoroughly convinced that if you require kids to do something inherently fun, you will immediately take the fun out of it and I will not be a party to anything that takes the fun out of reading.

A reading log is the biggest buzz-kill ever invented, and only serves to make kids think reading is just another school chore in their lives. It so effectively takes the fun out of whatever you have to log that I bet if you made your kids eat twenty M&Ms a day, *and* keep a log of it, by the end of a month they'd never eat another M&M again.

Now, as I said, I do *not* underestimate the value of reading. I'm aware that how much a kid reads is the number-one predictor of school success—which is why the academic world wants our kids to read, and thus hit upon the diabolical reading log.

I suspect I am not the only one out there who has fudged a reading log, but perhaps you are concerned that your kids won't read enough without it. So here, for those of you with kids young enough to still screw up, is what I did. It seems to have worked pretty well.

Read to them every day: I did this for Atticus from the time I brought him home from the hospital. Not kidding. I did it selfishly, because I liked it. I'd waited years to have a baby of my own on my lap to read to. When Grace came along, I read to one child and Jeff to the other. Every night. When Lilly was born, we got Atticus in on the act and he started reading to the girls. Now, of course, they just read to themselves but the fact is they do read. A lot.

***Never say no to reading**:* I also had a rule as they grew—no matter what, if they asked me to read to them, I would stop whatever I was doing and read. I would stop folding clothes to read *Noisy Nora*, or I would turn off the stove for *Good Night Moon*. It did not matter what I was doing, it was the one request I always honored.

Never say no to books: I never gave in when my kids begged for toys and candy at the store. My standard answer was, "Is it your birthday? Do you have money?" This works by the way; my kids only begged a few times before they learned it would not work. But I *would* buy them a book if they asked. I know this is a luxury, but you can substitute a trip to the library and you're good to go.

All three of my kids are avid readers— but it is not because of the stupid reading logs. It is in spite of them.

So I encourage you to fight the system a little, and

say no to some of the nonsense. Who knows, if we band together, maybe we can get rid of the word-searches and the map-coloring, too. A girl can dream.

Old Room-Mom

A couple of weeks ago I went to the local craft store in search of Valentine's Day craft crap. There was nothing there. Of course not, it was two days before Valentine's Day, why would I expect to find anything for that holiday? The store was already festooned with red, white, and blue bunting, and make-your-own American flag kits for Fourth of July, so why was I trying to find some last minute Valentine's Day crafts?

I was there because, for some reason I cannot remember, I volunteered to be a room parent again this year and it is my turn to run the Valentine's Day party.

I stood at a sale bin of half a dozen red foam thingies with two other slacker room-moms picking through the stuff listlessly. They looked as disinterested as I did so I suspect they are old hags like me who have been at this a little too long.

It doesn't help that this year I am paired with one of those annoying uber-room-moms (I'll call her URM) who wants to do everything to the *n*th degree. She is not familiar with the saying "less is more." In fact, she may not be familiar with the word "less." It is not enough for her to host a class party that merely has clever crafts, fun games, delicious snacks, and over-the-top decorations. No, that is her starting point. It's moms like her who get out of hand and lead to the unfortunate "everyone missed the Halloween party because the fire alarm went off when the smoke machine malfunctioned and the school had to be evacuated" incident of 2008.

URM was in charge of the Christmas party. She asked me to help. She was in the corner overseeing a craft project in which the kids made necklaces out of jingle bells (surprisingly a pretty good, low-key project). Before long I heard her voice rise sharply, "No, you need to stop now! You have *too many jingle bells*!" she was saying to a girl who was rather maniacally stringing a few dozen bells on her vinyl lanyard rope. A few more minutes passed and URM came over to enlist my help.

"What. Am. I. Supposed to do about this!" she hissed at me with barely contained fury.

"Excuse me?" I said.

"That girl! She's using too many jingle bells!" she said speaking of a tiny fourth-grader as if she had just knocked over a liquor store.

"Umm, ask her to stop?" I suggested.

"I did and she won't!"

"Alright," I sighed. "I'll play bad cop." I walked over and tapped the little felon on the shoulder. She looked up at me with Ritalin-laced-googley-eyes and I knew there would be no reasoning with her. "That's your last jingle bell," I said.

"I just have to finish this," she said, without malice. She was not naughty, she was crazy.

I went back to break the bad news to URM. "She doesn't mean to hog them; she's just fixated."

"Well!" she harumphed. "What will I tell the other children when they come to make a necklace and we're out of jingle bells?!" she demanded to know. I looked around the room. There was a karaoke machine in the corner, snacks on the table, gifts from the gift exchange in a pile, Nerf football in another corner, a Christmas video playing on the TV, and a rockin' game of Twister out in the hall. I looked at the clock. There was maybe ten minutes left before clean-up time.

I shrugged. "I don't know what you'll tell them. They'll be heartbroken if they can't make a jingle bell necklace."

Later URM sidled up to me and asked if she could help at the upcoming Valentine's Day party. No, I assured her, I had it all taken care of. She looked crestfallen and I was confused. I realized she wasn't offering to help just to be polite.

"You mean you actually *want* to attend?" I asked incredulously. I would rather try to wrestle a toddler into a snowsuit than attend a class holiday party.

"Yes, of course I want to attend!" and she looked at me strangely. "Why did you even volunteer to be a room-mom?" she asked.

Well, that stung a little. But she's right. Why am I a room-mom? And why am I making fun of someone who's doing her job well and taking it seriously and giving it the thought and time it deserves? Why am I making fun of someone who is serving so joyously?

I'll tell you why! I have room-mom burnout big time. I've been doing this for years and, frankly, I wasn't that good at it when I was ten years younger and gave a shit. I don't like coming up with crafts, I don't think kids need more treats, and actually, now that I think of it, I don't really like kids.

So I've decided to move on. Much to the relief of the room-moms and children everywhere, I bid you adieu. I'm passing the torch. Hanging up my brownie pan. Retiring my glue gun. You get the idea.

Good luck, and remember when it comes to room parties, more probably is more.

Screen Time

Yesterday I noticed a thoughtful post on Facebook by my friend Amy B. who is looking for software that would limit the time her children spend on the computer. Now that's a great idea, I thought, having failed miserably at prying my teenage son away from his virtual life, so I went to the website someone suggested and checked out some software. It sounded great and even gave this suggestion for how it might limit the time: "For example you might want to set up a schedule like this: Monday-Friday 5:30 p.m. to 7:30 p.m., with fifteen minutes allowed for their favorite game, fifteen minutes to chat and ninety minutes for homework."

After a half-hour or so when I could stop laughing doubled over, I went downstairs to the computer to find my son to read that line to him. We weren't sure which was funnier, the notion that he could limit his game time to fifteen minutes or the pie-in-the-sky dream that he would ever spend ninety minutes on his homework (with or without the computer). He was so amused he even lifted his hands off the keyboard and made eye contact with me. "Fifteen minutes on my game? What the fuh?" and then we started laughing again.

I am reminded of the time I bought new carpeting for the family room when the kids were five, four, and one. "Now," the salesman cautioned me, "you know you should vacuum once per week for every person in the household." I set the baby down, separated the two toddlers, wiped vomit off my shoulder, handed the baby a cracker, and then said to the five-year-old. "Quick, you do the math, how many times a week would I be vacuuming?" He's a smart kid (or was before all the computer time) so he answered quickly, "Five times, Mommy."

I wasn't trying to be rude when I laughed at the carpet salesman. He looked slightly offended when we all roared at the notion of mommy vacuuming five times a week. Even the one-year-old chortled as she ground her cracker into the floor-room sample of our future carpet.

So allow me to laugh when I read the suggested computer limits for my son. Because really, if there is one thing I've failed at as a parent — no wait there are many, many things I've failed at including getting my kids to eat fruits and vegetables as anything more than a condiment, and having them make their beds ever, and well, now I'm starting to depress myself — it is in the area of limiting screen time.

Make no mistake, I tried and I tried. And then I failed. But when I was still trying and we used to do that TV Turn-off Week, I was one of the few moms that actually included *all* screens. We went to the library. We played games. We rode bikes to the park all that week. Fat lot of good that did.

And I did move the computer into the kitchen as the experts suggest. That's helpful. I now can see the back of my kid's head at all times and view the ridiculous medieval war graphics on the game he's playing. I suppose this is a little like Mrs. Dahmer saying, "Well it's not that bad; I *saw* Jeffrey stacking up bodies in the backyard. What kind of mother do you think I am?"

When you learn about dog training you learn that it is almost impossible to get a dog to stop a bad behavior unless you distract him with the job of a good behavior. Which is why you will see me, from time to time, tell my computer-addicted kid to come empty the dishwasher or take the trash out or help his sister with her math. He always does this cheerfully and willingly, most likely because he is aware that it is the price he pays for being on the computer for hours on end, and he would be right.

So for now that's where we are on this issue. I think I will pass on the monitoring software because (1) I would actually have to have him install it and (2) I would then set it on such ridiculous levels — "No games after midnight or before 9 a.m." — that it might automatically dial a family services hotline and report me.

As for Amy, I wish you nothing but the best, and if you find some software that trains me to be a better parent too, just send me the link.

Part VI: All God's Creatures

Losing Nemo

When you go into any kitchen around here you will see a fish bowl with at least one goldfish swimming around inside of it. The reason you will see this is that everyone around here attends the annual PTA carnival at which the children of this suburb are given the opportunity to win a goldfish.

No parent really wants a goldfish but no parent wants to be the one to stand up at the PTA meeting following the spectacularly successful PTA carnival and say, "For the love of God can we lose the friggin' goldfish!" No. No one wants to be the killjoy to say that.

So year after year there are goldfish at the carnival. Every fall I troop off to the PTA carnival and despite my best efforts to distract the children, "Look, here's the clothespin drop, you could win a plastic parachute guy," they are lured by the siren call of the goldfish tank. It does not help that my husband is standing a few feet away saying, "Dude, forget the lame parachute guy. If you throw a ball in an empty applesauce cup, you win a *live fish*! Look, it's easy; even the first-graders are winning!"

Yes, my son was pleased as punch when he carried his new pet home in a baggie the night of that first fall carnival. The next day I was forced to go out and buy a goldfish bowl and food. What a racket. No wonder the pet store practically gives those fish to the PTA.

So now I found myself into the "free goldfish" for about twenty bucks. And guess who gets to clean the bowl? Not the bonehead who encouraged my son to win the goldfish. And no, not my son. No, of course not. Because despite the fact that I vowed when they brought the stupid fish home that it would be a good experience for my son, that it would teach him to be responsible, it turns out that his tolerance for fish scum is much, much higher than my tolerance. And so I found myself emptying the fish bowl and scraping that green gunk off the sides of the bowl every few weeks, which I didn't really enjoy.

Nevertheless, I felt sorry for the little guy swimming around all alone and I let my son talk me into buying the fish a friend. After all, no creature should be alone, and they only cost 10 cents at the pet store (not surprisingly the very same store that sells bowls), and it turns out you need a larger bowl if you have more than one fish — funny how that works. And so it went, month after month, me scraping the fish scum, me feeding the darn things because although I have no affection for them I certainly didn't want to see them starve to death, and my son not doing any of that.

Sometimes when we went on vacation, I hoped my neighbor would forget to feed the little devils and we could have a happy flush funeral. No such luck. My neighbor is alarmingly reliable.

One day I just couldn't take it anymore. I called the kids into the kitchen and pointed to the stupid fish. "Look, does anyone really care about these fish anymore?" The littlest started to protest but I hushed her. "I mean care enough to clean the bowl?" which was a bit of a trick question as it was at its murkiest and furriest at that moment. They remained mute. "Then no one will protest if I give them away?" They all agreed to that solution, in fact, looked relieved at the thought that I might stop nagging them about something they never had any intention of doing.

Now I had the nearly insurmountable task of trying to get rid of three — we'd been to another carnival — relatively healthy goldfish. The pet store didn't want them. None of my friends wanted them; they already have five or six of their own. I knew from watching

Finding Nemo that I couldn't really humanely flush them (who knows where they'd end up?) and even though I didn't care if they lived or died, I certainly didn't want to commit piscicide and then bury them out back. So I just kept feeding and scraping.

A few weeks later it was time for the fall carnival. I shook my head in dismay at the possibility that my problem could actually get bigger.

And then I had an idea. A brilliant, devious idea.

I got out an old Tupperware container and I filled it with water and put Pearly, Nemo, and Squiggley inside. I carried this container boldly into the fall carnival. My crime was surprisingly easy. I marched right up past the long line of children and doofus dads waiting to "win" a goldfish in a baggie. I slipped past the poor teenager who had been wrangled into running the booth that evening. I opened the container and dumped our fish into the tub with all the other goldfish. They looked much larger than the others but they also looked quite content. The teenager looked surprised. "Didn't your kid want his prize?" she asked.

I shook my head, pretending to be sad, "No, he won three but he doesn't want any."

A few weeks later I went to have a glass of wine at a neighbor's house. She was lamenting that her daughter won yet another fish at the carnival this year.

"It's strange though, this fish is like twice the size of the others," she said as I went to the bowl to look at the freakishly large, very familiar-looking fish.

I smiled but offered no explanation. The criminal mind is inscrutable. I just nodded in agreement and said, "That *is* strange," and held my glass up for a refill.

Dog Days of Spring

Well the day has finally come. It's my own fault because I once said, "I never want to become one of those dog-walkers," when I noticed that the moms with older kids all seemed to get dogs. I cursed myself just as surely as I did when I declared I would never use disposable diapers, which lasted about three days, or the time I vowed I would never live in Schaumburg but ended up living there four years. Once I say "never" it's sure to come to pass.

I had an inkling it was coming about a year ago when I was bragging to Val, over coffee, about how responsible my girls were with their new dog-walking business. They'd developed their own advertising, gotten a client, and faithfully walked the two dogs without having to be reminded. They took their earnings and bought toys for the dogs and gave the rest to an animal shelter. She looked me square in the eye and said, "You know you have to get them a dog, don't you?"

But I held out a long time. I held out nearly ten years under a constant barrage of begging for a dog. All kids are dog-obsessed at some point but my girls are like crazy dog-stalkers. They ask for a dog daily. If I say,

"Can I get you anything at the grocery store?" they say, "A dog." They own a dog collar, leash, bowl, and cage that they play doggie with. Every book they read, every movie they see is about a dog. Every wishbone, birthday candle, and loose-eyelash wish has been spent on wishing for a dog.

Yet I resisted. For all the usual reasons, I resisted. I told them that if they could find a dog that does not poop or shed or need to be taken out we could have it. For years I stuck to that. But alas, they have worn me down.

To put it succinctly, their desire to get a dog finally outweighs my desire to not get a dog.

I never had a dog as a kid. Well, we had a few but my mother always came up with reasons to get rid of them. Calhoun the beagle puppy chewed too much. Of course he chewed too much; he was a puppy. And Herbie the mutt was fine, but when we moved my mother managed to find a rental house that would not allow dogs. At least that's what she said. But it was OK because Herbie went to live on a nice farm. No, really. I think.

What can I expect from my mom though? Her own dog, Belle Star, had to be "put down" because she had mange. When that came up recently, I went to the encyclopedia to find out what mange is. Imagine my mother's disappointment to learn that her father had offed her childhood pet for having a bad case of dandruff. Ah, well, that's why we have therapists.

Anyway, we're all prepared for the new arrival. First we had to get rid of some of the stupid pets we've acquired over the years in my misguided effort to avoid getting a dog. In fact, it was the demise of dear Oreo the guinea pig that got me thinking of a dog at all. With her out the door (and buried in the backyard) that left only four stupid pets. I talked Lilly into getting rid of the parakeets (they went to live on a farm) and we now *only* have WonderBunny and Snuggles the guinea pig.

To prepare for our new arrival, we've begun talking as if we already have a dog. I frequently shout out, "Get that damn dog off the couch!" or "Tell Starbucks to get his nose out of my crotch." Lilly (just turned nine) gets into this game. I heard her yell, "Smokey, quit drinking from the toilet!" yesterday.

Today is the day. We will go to the shelter to see who needs us. The girls have been checking the shelter online daily and watch the dogs they want come and go but we just weren't ready until this week (too many travel plans). Yesterday they noted with chagrin that their No. 1

pup, Lenny the hound dog, was gone, apparently adopted over the weekend.

Grace was sad that we may have missed the perfect dog, but Lilly reassured her: “When we get there, God will make sure that the dog that was meant to be with us will be there.”

I like her faith. I’m sure we’ll find the perfect dog who needs us and in the end the perfect dog we need even more.

Let’s just hope he never develops a fatal case of mange.

Molly Finds Us

Before we got the dog I told anyone who would listen — and the surprising number who asked — what kind of dog we were looking for. Had to be a shelter dog. Had to be a mature dog so I didn't have to train it. Absolutely no puppy because puppies are such a hassle and blah, blah, blah. We went to the shelter the very first day it was possible for us to have a dog and we took a mature dog out for a test walk. He was great. He was calm, well-behaved, and very sweet. His name was appropriately — Placid. Lilly could walk him, which is the real test because she's not very big. She was sure she could handle a dog like that.

I was a little skeptical because the dog looked to be almost as big as Lilly. No, Lilly assured me, she could walk Placid no problem. Well, I countered, what if he saw a squirrel or something and took off. Again she assured me she could handle that. So we tested it. I had Grace throw a tennis ball. Placid, ignoring his moniker, took off like a shot, dragging Lilly around the shelter yard on her stomach, just like in the movies, while I helpfully screamed, "Oh, oh, oh!"

Grace, who has proven herself quite useful in emergencies, had the presence of mind to shout, "Let go of the leash!" which Lilly did. Fortunately, only Lilly's pride was truly wounded (and her knees and elbows a little).

We tried to walk two more mature dogs. But they were both very strong, muscular, and not well-behaved. I didn't even try to walk one of them, which was jumping up on me.

"See what you did," the trainer admonished as she led him back to his prison, which made me feel very bad for him.

Frustrated, I reluctantly took Grace's suggestion to at least check out the puppies. They led us to a small room with three crates. In one crate, three, tiny, tan puppies stood barking sweetly at us. I don't even know who was in the other two crates because Grace made a beeline for that crate of three and that was the end of that. Grace took one puppy out who immediately snuggled in her arms like a kitten with her head on her shoulder. Then I held her and knowing Grace as I do, accepted the fact that we were getting a puppy. "OK, which one of these three is going home with us?" Grace pointed to the shy one, now trying to hide in the corner. She had to reach way in to get her.

The whole time I filled out the paperwork — what the hell? There's less paperwork when you have a baby — and heard about our new dog's short life (she'd been picked up by Animal Control in Chicago with her four littermates at the age of seven weeks), the puppy sat on Grace's lap. She did not wiggle or bark or move except to snuggle closer to Grace.

In the car on the way home, Grace declared her name was to be Molly. That night, despite advice to keep her in her crate, I let her sleep with the girls. It's just too mean to take a puppy from its siblings and make it sleep alone. Everyone said puppies have to get up and go out at least twice a night, so the girls had flashlights and elaborate plans about who would get up and take her out first. But when I went to wake them up this morning, Molly was right where we'd left her, between them on the bed, waiting for her new girls to wake up and play with her.

Cicadas

This morning they were so loud they woke me up. I dreamed someone was using a power drill but when I awoke I realized it was the cicadas, already starting their daily drone.

The seventeen-year plague of cicadas is in full swing here in the Chicago suburbs. For those of you not enjoying this phenomenon of nature let me enlighten you: Cicadas are around every summer, they are that buzzy sound you hear on a hot August afternoon, but every seventeen years, a particular genus of cicadas that has been lying dormant, emerges all at once.

It is a biblical-looking event. There are so many that the sidewalks are covered with them and you cannot walk without stepping on one or several. They cover the bark of a tree so effectively that at first you think it is just the bark until you see that it is moving.

They are incredibly large bugs — about two inches long with goofy red, beady eyes. They crawl out of the ground at night as nymphs, climb up a tree, shed their shell, let their new wings dry out, and go find a mate.

After feasting underground on tree sap for seventeen years, they have no need to eat. Like crazed bachelors on a Vegas bender they have one thing in mind and they don't bother to stop to eat or sleep. Once they've mated, the male has a cigarette and dies with a smile on his face. The female finds another tree, burrows her tail into the bark, lays 600 eggs and then, exhausted and cranky, dies. Her eggs will hatch into ant-size nymphs that will fall from the trees like rain to burrow underground where they will wait for another seventeen years to repeat the process.

The Trib says there are about a million per acre out there. I think that number is low. Four and five cling to every leaf of our maple tree. For some reason they love my car tires and I find a dozen on each wheel every time I get into the car. They sun themselves on my back fence and as I type I see them whirring through the air of my backyard.

They started to come out exactly when the scientists told us they would, on May 22, which by sheer coincidence is the day we went to the shelter and got our new puppy, Molly. She finds them very tasty. The first time she gobbled one up I was appalled. They're still quite active when she eats them and sometimes if she opens her mouth too soon, they fly away. The paper says they are good protein and we should let the dogs eat them. As if I could stop her.

They came somewhat gradually. The first weekend, as we came out of church, I said, "Do you hear that?" It was a roar in the distance, not unlike the sound you hear when you leave the undergrad library at University of Michigan on a game-day Saturday afternoon. But by now, two and a half weeks into it, the sound is more like we live in the stadium. When we are outside we have to shout to be heard. They are more active now too as time is running out, flying in a frenzy from shrub to tree to car in search of each other like patrons in a bar when they turn the lights on.

I'm deathly afraid of bugs but I have become desensitized. The key is to not look too closely at anything. If you do, you will see them in Hitchcock-ian numbers crawling in the grass, littering the sidewalk, covering a plant. Driving down the street we see pedestrians doing The Cicada Dance as we've dubbed it: the crazed herky-jerky movements we do to shake one off when it lands on you. They don't bite or anything but they are so big they give you the willies if they land on you.

Yesterday, two of them were copulating on my windshield as I drove along. I kind of felt sorry for them as I flicked them off (they were distracting the driver). Imagine being underground for seventeen years, finally hooking up, and being tossed aside in midact by a windshield wiper.

It's been fun watching them and learning about them. The kids are experts on them and collect them and tell me the blue-eyed ones are rare and "valuable" (to whom I don't know). They are indeed an awesome display of nature. Coming up from out of the ground on cue. Like my neighbor says, how do they know to come out at seventeen years? Not sixteen, not eighteen, but seventeen? And what kind of life cycle is that? To only be above ground six weeks after being underground 878 weeks? Do they communicate while they're under there? Talk about what they're going to do when they finally see the light of day? I doubt that any of them plan to take their maiden flight and get eaten by a pup that has only been on earth nine weeks. What the hell kind of ending is that?

I think we're all growing rather fond of them and take pity on them for having such a desperately short life above ground. As Coffee Friend Steph says, "I even flip them over on their feet if they get stuck on their backs. I feel sorry for them. They deserve to find love."

They are also a reassuring reminder that despite alarming news of global warming and inane news of Paris Hilton, some things are constant and the cicadas will return in seventeen years.

When they come back our new pup will be an old seventeen-year-old dog, if she is still with us. Perhaps she'll gobble up a cicada and the sweet tickling sensation on her tongue will remind her with great fondness of her first summer on earth; her first summer with us.

Becoming a Dog Person

There was a movie in the sixties called *Charly* (based on *Flowers for Algernon*, a book we had to read in high school) about a mentally challenged man who, through some scientific process, was given the opportunity to become "normal." His intelligence grew and grew until he was a genius, learning languages and devouring books. Unfortunately, the science was faulty (go figure) and he learned (according to Wikipedia) that "the neural enhancement is only temporary, and he too is doomed to revert to his original mental state. He records his struggles to find a way to stop the decay until he realizes the futility of his situation. Charlie's writings gradually begin to reflect the recession of his intelligence. He becomes depressed when he realizes that he can no longer understand his own proof — the pinnacle of his genius phase. By the end of the story, Charlie's brain has returned to its initial state."

Anyhoo, I was thinking of this movie because I realize that sort of like Charlie, my brain is deteriorating — not because I had a brain operation but because I now own a terrier mix named Molly and my dog-hating brain is slowly morphing into the crazy putty that is a dog-lovers' brain.

So like Charlie, who journals as he loses his intelligence — quick, before I lose all my good sense — I will give you some insight into the dog world while I can still remember what it's like to be a dog-hater. I'll try to explain some of the stuff that dog-haters worry about so that you can understand why people love dogs so much. Let's address the obvious things:

Hair: You're wondering why a normally clean person would put up with all that goddamned hair in their house, on their couch, on their clothes, and in their car, aren't you? I know, you gag a little when you see a dog hair floating around anywhere near where you are going to eat. I know, because I was like that too. Well, let me explain. These buggers are hairy. It's really that simple. I now vacuum my house every single friggin' day at five, have two lint rollers lying around and one more in the car, and there is still hair all over the place. So unless I'm going to shave her, there you have it. Dog lovers put up with the hair because we have no choice.

Jumping: Before Molly, I absolutely hated going to houses of people who have dogs because they jump on you — the dogs, not the people. They jump up and dig their sharp claws into your legs and slobber on you — yuck! Well, I still hate that but now I have a dog that does it too! It turns out that it's really, really, really, really hard to train them not to do that. They are so desperately needy. They don't jump on us all day, they save that for the new person at the door. They just want you to love them like Madonna. They are needy, needy, needy. Short of a Taser or, as my father likes to say "a good swift kick with a boot" (both methods of discipline I loathe) it is difficult to break this habit. It requires immense discipline on the part of the owner. Even more discipline than *parenting* requires, for God's sake. My kids are much, much better behaved than this silly animal and they never jump up on the UPS man when he comes to the door, but as for Molly, well, I'm not sure we've made any progress on that front.

Wet Nose: Yes. They have one and it is always wet and they always insist on sticking it on your bare leg. Unless I cut it off (the nose not the leg), I see no solution for this one.

Smell: You know that “wet dog smell”? I thought that was just when they were wet or dirty. No, they pretty much smell all the time except when you bring them home from their expensive visit to the “dog groomer.” Good lord.

Barking: People talk, dogs bark. That’s life. Luckily, we have a quiet dog. If she were a human, she’d be an introvert and sit in the corner at cocktail parties watching all the others yak on. She will bark at first when you enter, but then you will not hear from her again. This is her nature so I am *very* happy to report, if you come over, you will not be subjected to endless yapping or barking. (You will however be jumped on, covered with hair, and have a cold wet nose stuck on your leg, but hey, stop by any time.)

In short, a dog is just as much of a pain in the ass to own as it would appear to those who don’t own a dog. So why do dog-lovers love their dogs so very much? Well, like all great loves it isn't very rational. It’s like babies — they really do cry a lot and poop their pants but we still keep having them and we’re pretty crazy about them too (most of us). She is a great companion to the children and very sweet and that does make up for a lot of the hair and other crap.

Still, the benefit-to-nuisance ratio is not tipping in Molly's favor.

But for now we'll keep her because she's the cutest little snookems who loves da mama, now don't you, my little pookie wookiee —

Help me, my mind is turning to mush. Before you know it I will dress her in a Santa hat and let her take food out of my mouth and put her on the Christmas card ... aaaagghhhh! I can't remember why I hate dogs. Maybe I need an operation to restore my brain. Must. Try. To. Remember. Why. I hate. Dogs.

House Bunny/Yard Bunny

We have a pet rabbit named WonderBunny who lives with us. He is fed and watered and taken to the vet on a regular basis. I often think how silly that is when I look at the bunnies in our backyard that run free. How little separates them from him. Though I worry about him and take him to the vet, I don't really do that for his little yard cousins.

This all came home to roost this weekend when Lilly found an injured baby bunny in the backyard. Something had already eaten the bunny siblings (we found the remains scattered around) and the mommy appeared to have abandoned her. Lilly begged to try to nurse her back to health. I knew how this would end but how could I explain the difference between caring for *our* bunny and caring for *this* bunny. Well, I couldn't really and I could not refuse her when she said, "But Mommy, I have to at least try to help."

And so we began the timeless ritual of finding a shoebox, feathering it with grass and fur and purchasing an eyedropper with which to feed the bunny. I made my stand on the issue clear, "I will buy the eyedropper but I will not take her to the vet!" I also informed her that I would not be buying kitten milk, which some website said a baby bunny needs and is available at your local vet. Who milks cats?

Drawing that line in the sand is a little odd. After all, I would buy WonderBunny kitten milk if he needed it to stay alive. I might buy a lactating cat to keep him alive.

It made me think of the kids at McNair Elementary. They're my own backyard bunnies, I guess. McNair is a school in a very bad part of Chicago that my Coffee Friends Val and Steph and I have adopted as our sister school. After railing against the disparities of education in this world — our kids have laptops, those kids don't even have crayons — we approached our principals about adopting an underprivileged school. They were all for it and we've been able to help out a little by sending them school supplies.

I send them crayons but I don't take them to the doctor. Another line in the sand. We do what we can and hope it's enough.

It was not good enough for the wounded bunny. She died yesterday and Lilly went into deep mourning, refusing to get out of her pajamas and bursting into tears all day long. She railed against a world that allows babies to get killed when they are just days old and I could not cheer her up much with talk of nature and the circle of life.

To make it even worse, when we looked out back at dusk we saw the mommy bunny. She'd come looking for her babies but they were all gone. The import of this moment was not lost on Lilly. She burst into tears again, "Would she would have lived if her mommy could have taken care of her? Is it my fault she died because I moved her? Should we take the body to her so she knows she's gone?"

I had no answers. Maybe the bunny would have lived if we hadn't tried to help. Maybe she wouldn't but the truth was I just didn't know.

Where to draw the line in the sand? When to help and not to help? When does our help do more harm than good? These are questions for all of us and they are not easily answered.

For now I guess I'll just have to stick with Lilly's initial response, "I have to at least try to help."

A Sheep in the Basement

My friend Ann R. grew up here in Glenview, which is close enough to the city to be more city than suburb. A hundred years ago there were a handful of farms but all that is left now is Wagner Farm, which our park district bought and runs so our kids can experience what we used to when we visited our grandparents: the smell of hay and manure, the sound of a rooster showing off for the hens, and the sweet lowing of milk cows, is all available for the price of a park district class.

Ann is a real city girl and did not even have grandparents with farms so her knowledge of animal husbandry is confined to Wagner Farm, which is why I imagine it was rather a surprise to her when her daughters expressed interest in joining the 4-H club, which meets — where else — at Wagner Farm.

She did not hesitate. She is a good mom — by which I mean she parents like I do, so it must be good — and she dutifully signed her girls up for 4-H. At the first meeting she learned that the kids would purchase an animal, take care of it for a year, show it at the state fair then sell it to a farmer and recoup most of their investment. Now when I say they will sell it to a farmer, I do not mean so the farmer can keep it in a petting zoo or as a pet. The farmer will do what farmers do and have the animal slaughtered for meat. (Come on, where do you think that Big Mac comes from?)

During that first year, they started small, with a sheep (they have since graduated to cows). They went every day in all kinds of weather to feed the sheep and muck out the barn. Her daughter Olivia was a tireless caregiver but since she can't drive yet that also means her mother was a tireless driver.

Things were going well until the sheep grew ill in the dead of winter and needed round-the-clock nursing. Since it was not possible for Olivia to sleep in the barn in the winter, Ann did what any good mother would do: She put the sheep in her car and took it home. It stayed one week in her finished basement until it was nursed back to health and returned to the farm.

The traumatic story of how they had to say goodbye to the sheep I will leave for another day. My point is, she let a sheep live in her basement for a week!

This is some sort of metaphor for parenting, I'm sure: One day you're pregnant and the next you have a sheep in the basement. At no point in the process before having kids do you think, "Gosh, what fun my kids will get me into! Maybe someday I can raise livestock in the media room." No. You really cannot see where these wonderful people will take you.

I love this part about being a parent, actually. It turns out that if you're really doing your job well and letting your kids be who they should be and not just some creation for you to live out your unfulfilled childhood, you will find yourself not just learning new stuff but learning stuff about stuff you didn't even know existed (4-H in Glenview?).

And this is how I found myself last night at an animal shelter in the city, sitting in a crappy concrete building, watching WonderBunny have a "bunny bonding" session with a girl bunny named SuzyQ (they're both fixed, get your mind out of the gutter). Because it turns out that if you want your bunny to have a partner — and Lilly makes a compelling argument for this — you need to first have your bunny spend time with the potential pal. So they meet in a caged-in area while a trained rabbit professional keeps them semi-separated with a special tool (a grease-spatter shield) so they can sniff each other but not bite or scratch. You must repeat the bunny bonding process several more times. Then and only then will the two buns bond. Who knew? Lilly did.

She'd done all the research and knew all of this ahead of time.

As I sat on the cold metal folding chair, watching the "bunny bonding" process and keeping an eye on the incontinent shelter cat who had already peed on my purse and reflecting on the many other ways I may have chosen to spend my Thursday evening, I thought to myself, "What the hell am I doing here?"

Then Lilly sidled up to me and whispered in my ear, "Oh, Mama, I'm so happy that WonderBunny will finally have a partner that I can't breathe. Thank you so much for bringing me here."

And I had my answer and I knew it was the same thing that compelled Ann, a city girl, to have a sheep in her basement.

Lunch with PETA Protesters

"Oh, hey, did you come for the protest?" asked the nice girl who had been packing up her car with the "Stop the McCruelty" signs. She leaned in through our car window.

"Yes. Well, she wanted to come," I said, nodding to Lilly in the passenger seat. We were parked along a secluded country road in Oak Brook, outside a gated community.

"Well, we're all done — I'm sorry. But we're about to go out for lunch. Can you join us?" she said with a big smile. I looked to Lilly for an answer. She was wearing her "Hell yes!" face so I turned back and said sure.

This is how I came to have lunch with four PETA protesters — complete strangers until that moment — a few Saturdays ago.

The girl in charge, who had introduced herself as Kate, closed her hatchback and went over to thank the police who had been assigned to keep the protest peaceful. They seemed like friendly guys, and she obviously had dealt with them before. I suppose it's no surprise that when the CEO of McDonald's lives on your beat, you know the animal-rights activists by name.

We followed Kate and two other cars to the mall and trooped up to a store directory board. "If we find a vegan-certified restaurant, I can expense it," Kate said, the only employee of PETA present (the rest were volunteers). As that would eliminate any restaurant that sold meat, eggs or cheese, I decided to intervene. I eyed up the four of them, pegged them all as vegetarians, possibly vegans (how much could they eat?), and made a quick decision.

"How about we just go to Cheesecake Factory and I'll pick up the tab?"

They were young, they were grateful, so we soon found ourselves looking at the world's largest menu. I was right; there were three vegans, two vegetarians including Lilly, and me, the carnivore. Watching them study the menu was kind of comical. To make it even more challenging, Kate, a vegan, was allergic to wheat and peanuts. That leaves, umm, not much. At last the vegans ordered veggie burgers, hold the mayo, hold the cheese.

We sat and chatted amiably. They were possibly the most earnest, sincere, kind, young people I've had the good fortune to spend time with in a long time. Kate, just a year out of college, had worked for PETA, her dream job, for just a few months. When she talked about Ingrid Newkirk, PETAs founder, she got breathless. Lilly had been hoping Ingrid would be at the protest, but no luck.

It's Kate's job to organize protests. She explained what it is she wants McDonald's to do: simply use a more humane method of killing their chickens. The method, she said, has even been recommended by an internal McDonald's' committee but no change has been made. We all agreed that the CEO, Jim Skinner, had an unfortunate last name given he was being accused of scalding and butchering animals alive.

The others, two women, and a man, were equally passionate about animal rights. Carmen, a brand-new protester, (she had agreed to wear the chicken costume despite the ninety degree temps), described the poor swans at her workplace that adorn the corporate pond. "They clip their wings so they can't fly away," she said.

"Horrific!" Kate said, looking a little like she might cry.

Lilly didn't say much, though her kindred spirits kindly tried to draw her out. Mostly she sat absorbing every word of the conversation with that contented look she gets when she is among other people who are as crazy for animals as she is. I've seen the same look on her face when she is at the bunny shelter. She loves crazy animal-lovers as much as she loves animals, and I have to say her affection is not misplaced.

I paid the check and hoped that somehow this counted as doing something good. Later Lilly thanked me. "We're changing the world, Mom." And I hope she's right, because I have come to believe that though there is nothing immoral about eating another creature, it is most certainly immoral to torture it before you do.

Part VII: Passages

What Will You Do All Day?

My youngest started first grade today and all week long everyone I run into says, "What will you do with your free time now?" A lot of people ask this in jest, knowing full well there isn't much you can do with the few hours when all the kids are out of the house at once.

Others ask in earnest knowing that a world of possibilities has just opened up. I have some ideas. I'm going to start exercising again. I'm going to write more. I'm going to finish my novel. Some of my friends will go back to work. Others will fill up the time doing more around the house, taking part-time jobs, or volunteering even more of their time to the schools.

It is strange but as a stay-at-home mom, if you do your job really well, you are rewarded by having your job taken away from you little by little. Today I was demoted to part time. It's not a huge chunk of time: nine to two-thirty due to staggered start times among my three children, but nevertheless it's a much bigger chunk of time than I've had in eleven years.

It's not a total shock of course. The free time comes quite gradually really, from the crazed frenzied days of breastfeeding and diaper-changing to the slightly less frantic days of potty-training and preschool schedules to the relative calm of kindergarten and early elementary days. But some parts of it are not so gradual. Like today, the first day of school. It's a wrenching change in my life.

My youngest is the best of my three children at expressing herself. This makes parenting her sometimes easier and sometimes much more challenging. Last night, she sat in my lap as I read *The Kissing Hand* and as I struggled to get through that tear-jerker she interrupted me to say, "Mama, I am not ready for first grade."

"What do you mean?" I asked prepared to give her a pep talk, to remind her that her best friend is in her class, she has the same bus route as last year, and she can already read chapter books.

"I'm not ready to be away from you for so many hours," she said simply. This stopped me dead in my tracks because the truth is I'm not really ready to be away from her for so many hours either. I mean maybe more than the two-and-a-half hours of a kindergarten day, but I really don't need her to be gone from me more than seven hours, which is what it turns out to be with the bus ride to and from school. Can't they have a four-hour day in first grade while we all adjust?

My eyes filled with tears but I turned my head so she could not see. I forced a cheerful answer, "But honey, you were gone that many hours just yesterday with Margaret when you went to her house and then to the movies and you didn't mind that."

"But I can't be away from you that many hours every day," she countered.

Now I began to cry in earnest, thankful that children seldom look their moms in the eye, and as I sat with her in my lap trying to compose myself, I most unhelpfully remembered a Dave Barry column in which he drives his son Rob to kindergarten for the first time and as they sit in the car outside the school saying goodbye, Rob asks, "Daddy, how long do I have to do this?" and he can't bring himself to answer, but he thinks, "Forever and ever." (I am paraphrasing from memory: apologies to Mr. Barry if I got this wrong.) I remember crying when I read that column and I didn't even have children then.

I shook my head trying to get the image of Rob and Dave Barry out of my head, and to distract myself I tried to figure out how old Rob must be now. He probably has kids of his own, and not nearly as close to his father as he was when he was five. That was no help so I lifted Lilly off my lap and told her I'd be right back.

I went into the bathroom and closed the door and sobbed into a bathroom towel. I was thinking of all the other mothers in my town, in my state, and probably in the world doing the same thing; crying into a bathroom towel because who else can you cry to? If only we had some acceptable way to share our collective grief, maybe it would help but parenthood demands we act cheerful and even relieved when our little ones begin to leave the nest.

For the most part we are relieved. But we are grieving too. So please remember that when you see us looking a little dazed at the bus stop in the morning or a little eager for the bus in the afternoon. Do not be deceived by our breezy answers to your question, "What will you do with your day now that the kids are all in school?" Because we're not really sure ourselves. Oh, we have lots of ideas, but we are afraid that any of them will pale in comparison to the wondrous job we are leaving behind: the privilege of caring for a little one 24/7.

Christmas Pageant

Yesterday was the annual children's Christmas pageant at church, and I can think of no other event that so clearly marks the passage of time. One minute your kids are among the preschoolers wearing sheep heads and donkey ears. You blink, and they're an angel or a shepherd, and after what seems like a few more weeks, they're playing the big parts of Mary and the wise men. This year the only one of my children still young enough to be in the pageant was Lilly, a real sign that my kids are growing up fast.

This event had it all: a cow who succumbed to a fierce bout of stage fright and burst into tears upon seeing the audience; a donkey who looked annoyed and tried to soothe the cow; adult wranglers who had to go up to the altar and lead the cow to safety; a bossy angel (daughter of the children's choir director) who, exasperated to find a mic missing just before Mary's solo, stomped off the altar in search of a replacement saving the song just in time; and we had the perfect, tear-inducing solo, sung sweetly by Mary.

Oh, did I mention Lilly was Mary?

When I went to pick her up from rehearsal on

Saturday the pageant director shared with me that Joseph (an eighth grader) had suggested he put his arm around his wife when she arrives at the manger. You can't blame a guy for trying. I mean, here he has gone to the trouble to bring Mary safely to the warm stable, and not only does he get no credit for the birth thing, but he has not one line in the Christmas play. Surely he had something to say that night like, "Can I get you some ice-chips?" During the rehearsal, this Joseph tried to slip his arm around Lilly/Mary but she just shrugged it off without looking up from her script. I certainly hope the first Mary was much more kind to Joseph.

I have seen many Christmas pageants over the years, from the very modest to the slickly produced, but I always prefer the slightly messy ones where angels' wings get tangled (one year a set of wings was set on fire), sheep heads slip askew, and wise men get a fit of giggles. A show that is far from perfect, but is kid-friendly, and full of hope and promise, just like the first Christmas at the manger.

Whatever kind of pageant you get to enjoy this year I hope it moves you to smile and be thankful for all the children, Sunday school teachers, church-lady seamstresses, and choir directors who bring us this little piece of magic every year.

School Days

It's back to school this week in Glenview and as I drive Grace to junior high, I wait behind a school bus that has stopped to pick up a young child. The mother and father are both there as it is the first day of school and I guess the first day of kindergarten judging by how wistful mom looks and anxious dad is. Dad places his hands on the child's shoulders as if he could hold him back from getting on that bus and maybe keep him a moment longer in the preschool world. I know what the parents are thinking. How quickly it went! Wasn't it just yesterday they were in the hospital with that newborn wondering how on earth they were going to take care of this new wondrous creature? Finally, the parents kiss him goodbye and reluctantly let go as he boards the bus with confidence. The bus pulls away and I'm not sure there's a more forlorn sight than that of the parents left behind.

I glance at Grace sitting next to me. Goodness, she's nearly a full-grown woman. She wears her new skinny jeans and has a new hairstyle with bangs that hang in her eyes. How did this happen? Wasn't it just a few days ago that she was in her new denim skirt, the one she picked out with Jeff on that special shopping trip in the city as they prepared for her first day of school?

Back at home Lilly is ready to head out to her elementary school. She has a backpack shaped like an alligator and wears her bike helmet without being reminded. She waves and pulls away from me, happy to meet her friend and ride to school. How could this have happened? Wasn't it just a few weeks ago that I told Atticus and Grace that they were going to have a new baby brother or sister?

As I turn to go back in the house I see my neighbor Ralph come out of his house. He's an attorney who works in the city and takes the train every morning. He and his wife, Gundy, are now the senior members of our block at the age of seventy. He sees Lilly riding down the street and he stops and watches her for a moment longer than I expect him to. His face grows dark with something that looks like grief and I know what he is thinking. How could Lilly be riding her bike to school already? Wasn't it just a while ago that Kurt, his fifty-year-old son, used to ride his bike down this same street to that same elementary school?

I wave at Ralph but he is lost in reverie and does not see me. I turn to go inside and get my coffee before the gravity of the moment can move me to tears.

And so it goes and so it goes.

The First

Superman's in pajamas on the couch
Goodnight moon, will find the mouse
And I love you

Godspeed, little man
Sweet dreams, little man
Oh my love will fly to you each night on angels wings
Godspeed
Sweet dreams

— *Godspeed,* Dixie Chicks

Last night as I lay in savasana, the resting pose at the end of yoga class, listening to a sweet lullaby with the words "Superman's in pajamas on the couch" and "Godspeed, little man," I was horrified to feel tears slip from beneath my closed eyelids. What the hell? I have heard of these moments in yoga. Apparently, opening up all your joints can open up your heart, and feelings you didn't even know you had come spilling out.

I asked myself, in good yogic fashion, now where is this coming from? Just observe. As usual, the answer came loud and clear.

I was crying about my own little man in the superman pajamas.

It wasn't just the song that made me cry, it was the revelation that my little man is no longer my little man. This thought was revealed to me not through this song but as so many revelations are, through the convergence of several seemingly random but cosmically connected events that happen in a small period of time. It just took the song for me to link them all together.

The chain started the other day when I came across the book I used to keep when the kids were all much younger filled with the clever things they say and I found this exchange I'd written down when he was just three. He said, "Mommy, I don't want to go to sleep."

"Why?" I asked him.

"Because if I do I'll grow and then I'll be taller than Daddy and he won't be able to give me a ride on his back."

Reading this made me smile. It is just within the past year that he has indeed grown taller than his daddy and of course much taller than me. It is a strange thing when your child grows bigger than you. He is, after all, your child for life, but only smaller physically for a shockingly small portion of your time together.

Then yesterday, I had the chance to babysit for my new neighbor across the street. She has a three-year-old boy and a baby girl. She needed to go to the boy's nursery school conference. "Who is his teacher?" I asked her.

"Carol."

That's the same teacher Atticus had when he was three. "Tell her I said hello."

I spent a delightful half-hour with Rohan, trying to keep his baby sister from rolling off the couch just like I used to with Atticus and Grace. We read books and sang *Itsy Bitsy Spider* and he told me I sang the words wrong and of course it all reminded me of Atticus at that age. He was a most delightful toddler.

You know, I have had a blessedly, over-the-top happy life, but I count among my happiest moments the time I spent alone with Atticus when he was a baby. That tiny window when it was just the two of us, from his birth to the birth of Grace eighteen months later (which was also blissful but instantly turned everything chaotic), was absolutely magical. I have known few things as sweet as sitting on the couch in the afternoon with him while he enjoyed a bottle of milk and we watched *Jeopardy* together. And why not? We were madly in love and damnit I miss that time. We only get to fall in love a few times in life, why is it always so darned short?

I guess all of this is why I was crying into my ears in yoga and grateful the room is dark and our eyes are closed. Because I am losing one of the great loves of my life. Even though he still lives here and he still loves me, the early days of being smitten with each other are long gone. He still laughs at my jokes sometimes but he is just as likely to scowl too. And even though I know some of that will change when he outgrows puberty, I am not kidding myself. Boys move on and out of their mother's lives, as it should be.

The song ended and I composed myself before the lights came back on. But I've been walking around grieving for the past day because I know now that my little man in the superman pajamas is long gone and he isn't coming back.

Godspeed little man.

Made in the USA
Lexington, KY
06 October 2016